Adventures in Hiking

A Young Peoples' Guide to the

Adirondacks

Adventures in Hiking

A Young Peoples' Guide to the Adirondacks

Barbara McMartin

Illustrated by Gregory Palestri

North Country Books
Utica, New York

Published by North Country Books, Utica, New York 13501

Copyright 1993 by Barbara McMartin

Library of Congress Cataloging-in-Publication Data

ISBN 0-925168-25-4

For the next generation of hikers,

the grandchildren,

Ali, Casey, Lisa, and Dan

With thanks to Jim Dawson and Courtney Young, hiking friends who read this book and made important suggestions; to Lee Brenning for trail information; to Nancy Young for editing the manuscript and checking the level of the text from the perspective of a reading specialist; to Greg Palestri, whose charming sketches invite young people to hike in the Adirondacks; and to my husband, Alec Reid, for creating the sketch maps.

Adventures in Hiking
A Young Peoples' Guide to the Adirondacks

Dear Reader,

You can use this guide to learn the basics of hiking and at the same time sample the great Adirondack Park. Use it as an invitation to take your parents or older friends and relatives hiking. This book will show you the fundamentals of protecting yourself as well as the plants and trees and animals that make hiking in the Park so rewarding. Hiking is a lot of fun, especially when you are in charge, and this guide will help you to take charge of all your adventures in the out-of-doors. You can be the one to introduce your family and friends to the best way to enjoy the Adirondack Park.

Happy hiking,

Barbara McMartin

The circled numbers correspond to hikes described in the guide. Directions for driving to their trailheads start on page 101. Dots locate alternate hikes.

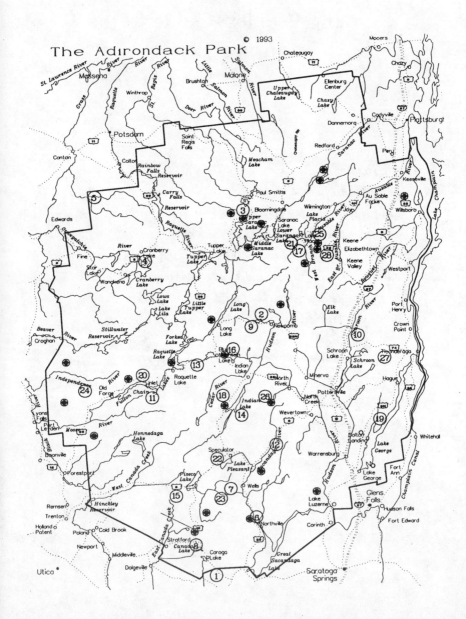

Contents

Getting Started

Hiking is a special kind of walking; it's walking with a purpose-to exercise, to discover new adventures, to reach a special place, to share time outdoors with friends, or to explore nature's wonders. Hiking is fun-and easy-almost as easy as the alphabet. In fact, A-B-C-D-E is about all you will need to get started.

A - Always hike with older friends or relatives; use this guide to introduce your mother or father to hiking. **Never hike alone.** A few of the trails in this guide may be near your vacation spot, but usually you will need someone to drive to the beginning of the hikes. Companions are for safety as well as for sharing the fun of the great out-of-doors.

B - Be sure someone who is not hiking with you knows where you plan to go and how long you will be gone. In case you have a problem, that person can tell the police or the Department of Environmental Conservation Forest Rangers.

C - Carry out what you carry in, never litter. The forests belong to all of us, so help keep trails clean and, if you can, pick up trash left by the few who are careless hikers.

D - D is for day-pack; a small backpack, properly filled, should always go with you. Properly filled means not putting too much in it; a heavy pack can spoil a trip. It also means taking a few necessary items. Start with a few important things and add what you discover you will need.

Important items for your day-pack include:

A plastic or light metal bottle for carrying water; juice boxes or aluminum cans will do, just remember to bring them back. You always need something to drink when you are hiking. *Never carry your liquids in glass containers because they can break.*

A snack or picnic lunch, depending on how long you will be hiking.

A rain jacket or light water-repellent wind breaker. Try to start out only in fair weather, but remember the weather can change. When you start climbing mountains, you will want a sweater, and for the really big climbs, you will need gloves and a hat, but that is for later on.

A small zip-lock bag with toilet paper or Kleenex.

A small bottle of bug repellent.

A map or a copy of the pages from this guidebook will be needed after the first few easy hikes.

Someone in your group should carry a small first aid kit. Adults who hike usually have bandaids and first aid cream in their kits. Someone in your group should also carry a small plastic shovel to bury body wastes. See page 62.

Later on, you will want a compass, so you can start learning how to use it. Along with the compass, you will want United States Geological Survey maps to guide you to new places.

You may want to carry a whistle, but do not depend on it to call friends, for the forest muffles sound. When you begin hiking longer hikes, you may also want to carry a small flashlight.

As you discover what interests you most about hiking, you may want to carry a camera or binoculars, or a book to help you identify the plants or birds or animals you see. But don't start with these-remember a light pack with the essentials is all you really need.

E - Equipment, fancy hiking equipment, is not essential at first. Of course, you do need a good pair of sneakers, high-tops preferably for ankle support, comfortable and well-worn. Later, when your feet stop growing, or when you venture on longer and steeper trails, or when you need to carry a heavier pack, you will want a good pair of hiking boots, but by then you will have had enough experience to know what will suit you best.

Just be sure that your sneaks or boots fit well. Make sure they are comfortable with plenty of room for your toes. Do not start out on a long hike with new sneakers or boots; wear them enough to be sure they do not make blisters. When you start climbing mountains, make sure your boots hold your feet tight enough so that your toes do not jam into the front of the boot when you walk downhill.

Summer is the Best Time to Hike

Start hiking during the late spring, after school is out, or during the summer or early fall. In the Adirondacks, springtime means black flies and these pesky little bugs can spoil any trip. Wait until late June when the black flies are almost gone. Then, with bug repellent, you can deal with them and with summer mosquitoes. Mosquitoes are most apt to bite early in the day or toward evening. In the middle of the day in summer, you probably will not need any bug repellent, but it is wise to have some in your day-pack.

Hiking in early fall is beautiful, but late fall is the time for hunters. It is best to avoid the woods after late September, or hike trails like the one to Goodnow Mountain where no hunting is allowed.

Winter is beautiful; instead of hiking you can snowshoe or cross country ski on many Adirondack trails. Winter can also be a dangerous time. You need special equipment and training for winter hiking. So, summer is the best time to start hiking in the Adirondacks.

About This Book

This hiking guide contains descriptions of twenty-eight different hikes. They are spread throughout the Adirondacks so you can learn about all the parts of this great Park. The person who drives you to the beginning of the trails will need a good road map. All the directions to the beginning of the hikes are at the back of this guide and each has a small sketch map to supplement your road map. The map I use is the *DeLorme Atlas for New York State*, which shows many of the trails as well as the roads leading to them. It is sometimes harder to find the beginning of trails than to follow the trails themselves. Start using the Atlas or an Adirondack region map so you can begin to understand maps. You can be the navigator on the way to the hikes.

The trails are grouped according to the kinds of places they will lead you. Accompanying each hike are definitions or bits of information on subjects important to Adirondack hikers. You can identify this information because it appears in a box. Before you go on to use other guidebooks, you should be familiar with the information in all of the boxes. This book breaks the information into small subjects to make each more easily understood, and each subject is introduced by a hike so that you can understand it better. All the new words and ideas you will use are indexed at the end of the book.

Some of the trail descriptions contain information about the trees and plants and rocks you will see. By the time you have done all the walks described, you will know many of the common Adirondack trees.

The maps in this guide are all reproduced from the United States Geological Survey maps and they are adequate for all the hikes described.

Along with the groups of hikes is a list of thirty-six similar hikes in other parts of the Adirondacks. A few have short descriptions so you can do them without further guides, others need more details and these can be found in my other guidebooks. You may want to start collecting USGS maps for the area you plan to hike in most often. Getting to the beginning of all the trails described in this book involves a lot of driving. If you live near or vacation in one part of the Adirondacks, you might want to have the corresponding guide from my *Discover* series to help you substitute alternate hikes in the different groups. See page 110 for a map showing the regions covered by the books in the *Discover* series. A number of the alternate hikes mentioned are also described in my *Fifty Hikes in the Adirondacks*.

You will find that there is quite a bit more to learn than A-B-C-D-E, but it is easier to learn it as you hike, so let's start.

1 Boardwalks and Nature Trails

Nature trails are short trails in special areas that can teach you a lot. The best nature trails go through a variety of places-deep woods, open fields, and wet areas. A few outstanding nature trails have boardwalks to carry you right out over the wet areas so you can see the birds and plants and insects that live in or near the water without getting your feet wet.

1 - Willie Marsh

The first hike is in the very southern Adirondacks. The nature trail begins across the road from the parking area. Walk a few feet down the path to the trailhead. Be sure to sign in at the trail register. Spend some time studying the painted trail map so you can figure out where you will be going and what to look for on the way.

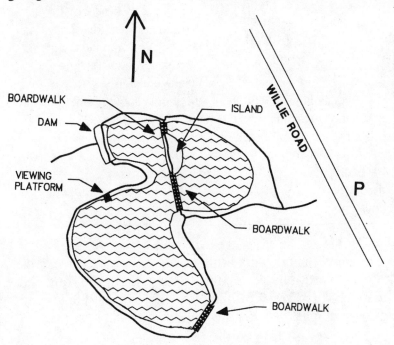

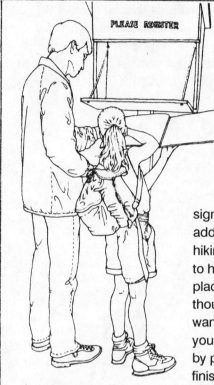

Trailhead is the term hikers use for the beginning of the trail. This guidebook tells you how to drive to the trailhead. Most trailheads have a **trail register**, a wooden box with a notebook and pencil inside.

There is room for you to sign your name and give your address. Put in the date you are hiking and how long you expect to hike. Sometimes there is a place for you to write what you thought of the trail. You might want to add a note about what you enjoyed when you sign out by putting down the time you finish your walk.

Registering is important. It lets people know where you plan to go and it lets the people who manage the trails know how many people are hiking along them and if people enjoy them.

This trailhead has a **map** of the trails you will follow. Not all trailheads have such maps. Most trailheads have a **guideboard**-a sign that tells you where the trail is headed and how long the trail is.

Willie Marsh trails are arranged in the shape of a figure eight. Plan to walk both loops, that way you will cross the long boardwalk twice. Start to the right of the trailhead and in just a few steps turn left. The narrow path takes you close to the marsh so you are walking on a spongy moss, called *sphagnum*, that holds a lot of water. This part of the trail may be wet. In just a few minutes, you reach a trail intersection. Turn right to the long boardwalk that leads out into the marsh. Stop and look for birds and bugs. At the end of the boardwalk, the trail crosses a small island and reaches a second shorter boardwalk over the water. Just beyond there is a trail intersection. The red trail forks left. After you have walked the long red loop, you will come back across the boardwalks again to the intersection and turn right on the yellow trail that will take you back to the beginning. If you only want a short walk today, you can turn right and head back now.

For the longer loop, do not turn right but walk straight ahead on the red trail, which takes you through a beautiful forest and curves around the end of the marsh. You walk across the narrow earthen dam that has raised the water to flood Willie Marsh. Beyond the dam, the trail makes a right turn into the forest again, then still circling the marsh, it crosses a part of it on a third stretch of boardwalk. Beyond that is another short forest walk and then you come to the trail intersection by the long boardwalk. Cross it again, this time turning right to return on the yellow trail, which winds around some wet places. Look sharp for the trail markers so you stay on the trail.

Trail markers come in different colors, sizes and shapes. Most hiking trails are marked with either yellow, red, or blue round disks. Snowmobile trails have larger orange disks. Some trail markers have writing that tells who put them up. Most of the trails you will hike with this book have been marked by the **New York State Department of Environmental Conservation** or **DEC**. That is the part of our government that is responsible for our trails and takes care of most of our forests.

2 - Adirondack Visitor's Interpretive Center

at Newcomb

The Adirondack Park has two Visitor's Interpretive Centers where you can learn all about nature in the park. The nature center at Newcomb has several loops of trails that circle a peninsula in Rich Lake or follow a stream. The trails take you to wet places, across marshes, through deep forests, up and down rocky knolls, and past an enormous beaver dam. You can spend several hours walking the trails at Newcomb or visiting the exhibits in the Visitor's Center, so pack a lunch and plan a whole day there.

First head down from the south side of the Visitor's Center on the Rich Lake Trail. The paved zigzags make the first part of this route wheelchair accessible. Cross the bridge with its first views of Rich Lake and Goodnow Mountain. The Rich Lake Trail makes a 0.6-mile loop. Take the right branch and be sure to look for mounds of shells of fresh water clams on the shore.

The trail takes you past a giant **glacial erratic**, a boulder that has been carried from a distant place to this spot by the glacier. Glaciers last covered the Adirondacks about eleven thousand years ago. The advancing ice sheets scoured the sides of mountains, picked up rocks and gravel and even moved large boulders. As the glaciers retreated, they deposited sand along the shores of lakes such as the lovely sand beach you see here at Rich Lake.

Near the erratic, the 0.9-mile Peninsula Trail branches from the Rich Lake Trail loop. Follow it west to an intersection. Part of the Peninsula Trail is also a loop. If you go left, you begin to climb the steep bluffs that border the peninsula. As you loop around the peninsula, you descend two sets of stairs, one of them built to take you down a small cliff. Then the trail finishes curving back around the shore to the intersection by crossing a wide marsh on a long boardwalk.

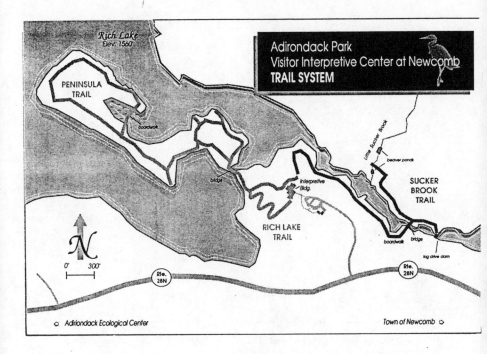

Retrace your steps to the beginning. You can spend as much as an hour and a half walking the 1.5-mile combined loop described.

For the second part of the walk, head out again from the Center, this time toward the 0.8-mile long Sucker Brook Trail. It takes you downstream beside the brook to a bridge. Cross the bridge and turn left. The trail crosses more wetlands, reaches a bridge over Little Sucker Brook, and from it you can see a large beaver dam. Turn around here and retrace your steps, completing about 0.8 mile in under an hour.

Did you notice a difference between the trails here and at Willie Marsh? There is a great difference between places in the Adirondacks and some of these differences are shown by the various types of trees you will find.

cedar

Notice the evergreen trees on the shores of Rich Lake. The most common here are called northern white cedar. You will not find them in the southern Adirondacks. They are medium-sized evergreens, 40 to 50 feet tall, with scale-like leaves in flattened sprays.

Stop at the Visitor's Center and look at a picture of cedar trees and perhaps you can learn what animals are dependent on their twigs and seeds for food.

Notice that the trail **map** has an arrow pointing to the top of the map. Our maps usually point north. Stand at the Visitor's Center and use your **compass** to find north. Hold your map so it points north too. What direction should you take to begin the Rich Lake walk? What is the direction of the long, marsh boardwalk? What direction do you take to reach the beginning of the Sucker Brook Trail? In which direction does Sucker Brook flow? When you turn left after you cross the bridge over Sucker Brook, which way are you headed?

Suppose there were no signs to tell you which trail to take. Could you find the trail you want with your compass? As you hike, stop occasionally and figure out which direction the trail is heading.

3 - The Adirondack Visitor's Interpretive Center

at Paul Smiths

A number of trails go out from the Visitor's Center. A favorite is the short Heron Marsh Trail that has boardwalks leading out into the marsh.

This time, look at the map and see if you can chart your own route. Start on the Heron Marsh loop, south of the Interpretive Building. Take the side closest to the marsh and after following it for 0.4 mile, you come to a bridge. You can choose to make the 0.6 mile loop on the Shingle Mills Falls Trail for a slightly longer walk. Today, cross the bridge and begin the 1.2-mile walk on the Forest Ecology Trail. This

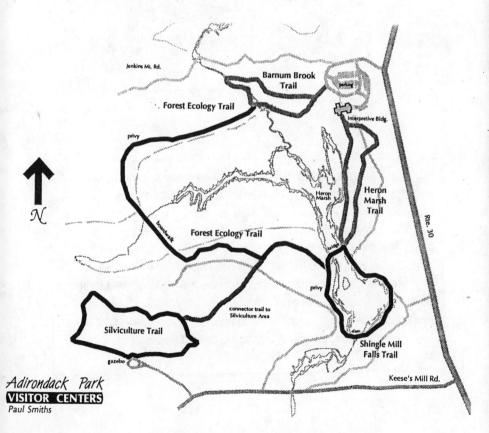

has a 250-foot long floating bridge. Notice the sugar maple exhibit. Can you identify a sugar maple by its leaves? Can you find red maple trees on your walks? Red maples grow in very wet places.

The Forest Ecology Trail leads to the Barnum Brook Trail where you can turn either right or left. It, too, is a loop, and either way leads back to the parking area.

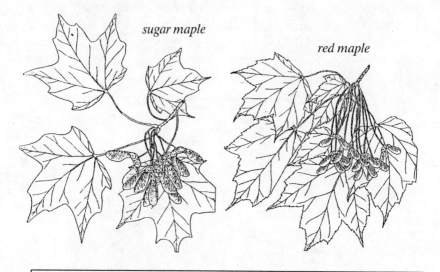

sugar maple

red maple

The Visitor's Center is a good place to see what other books you might want to have someday to help you learn about the nature trails you are walking. There are books on flowers and ferns, trees and shrubs, birds and mammals, butterflies and bugs. It is fun to pick one part of nature and learn all about it on your hikes. This book will help you get started with the trees.

Remember that most of the wild flowers you see and almost all the ferns are **protected**. That means that you cannot pick them, so leave them there for all to enjoy. As you walk around Paul Smiths' trails, count how many different flowers you see. Make a list of the ones you know.

4 Cranberry Lake Boardwalk Nature Trail

A new trail heads east from the Cranberry Lake Public Campground. The trail is 2.1 miles long and you have to return to the start, making a 4.2-mile trip. You can turn around at any point for a shorter walk, but you will want to go at least as far as the second of the 250-foot-long boardwalks. One crosses a part of Bear Mountain Swamp and the other is near some recent beaver work. You should turn around and walk back when you reach the red-marked Burntbridge Pond Trail and the end of the nature trail. Along the walk are thirty-four numbered stops with black numbers on orange disks. Each number corresponds to a

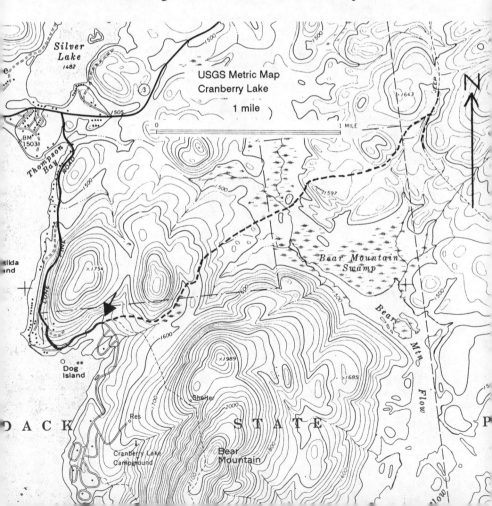

USGS Metric Map
Cranberry Lake

1 mile

description in a guide, which you can obtain at the Campground entrance, where you will have to pay a day-use fee.

All of the typical Adirondack trees, many of the wild flowers, and a sampling of ferns line the trail. If you can identify the plants listed in the guide to the boardwalk, you will be able to appreciate most Adirondack trailsides.

Other Nature Trails and Boardwalks

There are not many other nature trails and boardwalks in the Adirondacks, and that is unfortunate because they are the best places to start hiking.

Silver Lake Bog is in the northern Adirondacks near Silver Lake. It has a boardwalk that takes you to a real bog. Chapter 7 lists some more bog hikes and tells why they are so special. To find this trail which is in an Adirondack Nature Preserve, drive one mile west on Union Falls Road from its intersection with Silver Lake Road, then turn right for 0.2 mile to the trailhead.

Pack Forest north of Warrensburg has a mile-long nature trail with a short boardwalk, a lake for canoeing, and marshes to explore by water. Pack Forest, managed by SUNY School of Environmental Sciences and Forestry, is on the west side of NY 9, north of the intersection of NY 9 and 28. The highlight of the hike through deep pine forests is the 'Grandmother Tree,' the tallest pine and the tallest tree in New York State. The marshes support nesting heron, ducks and beavers.

Raquette Lake Railroad is not an official nature trail, but the raised bed of the abandoned railroad provides a raised walkway through bogs and wetlands in the western Adirondacks. The railroad bed is marked as a snowmobile trail and it starts as an extension of Dillon Road, which is near the Library in Raquette Lake and heads west to Brown's Tract Road near the eastern end of Upper Brown's Tract Pond.

II - Waterfalls

The Adirondacks is a special place because of its combination of lakes and streams with mountains. This combination does not exist in any other place in the United States. There are thousands of miles of rivers and streams and many of these have beautiful waterfalls. The hikes to those waterfalls are among the best in the Adirondacks.

A hundred years ago, a few Adirondack forests had been very heavily cut. Several years were much dryer than normal and there were severe forest fires. If forests are too heavily cut or become too dry, whatever rain falls can drain away quickly and streams become dry. Preserving the flow of water in Adirondack rivers and streams was one of the reasons that New York State decided to preserve Adirondack forests. To do this, the state acquired many thousands of acres of forest land. This land is owned by the state and anyone can walk on it. That is why we sometimes call it **public land**.

The Constitution of New York State says that no trees can be cut on the public land in the Adirondack Park. We sometimes call the patches of public land that are scattered throughout the Adirondacks the **Forest Preserve**.

Most of the trails in this book are in the Forest Preserve. A hundred years ago, in 1892, the state government took a map and drew a blue line around the Adirondack region. Most of the patches of Forest Preserve were inside the oval blue line, which was the first boundary of the **Adirondack Park**. Since then, the blue line has been extended so that it now looks as it does on the map on the next page, where the public lands are shaded.

Not all the land within the blue line is Forest Preserve. People live and work on **private lands** within the Park. Lumbermen can cut trees on the private lands. People build houses and summer homes on the private lands. There are villages with schools and churches and hospitals within the Adirondack Park. This makes our Park different from those, like Yosemite, where all the land is publicly owned.

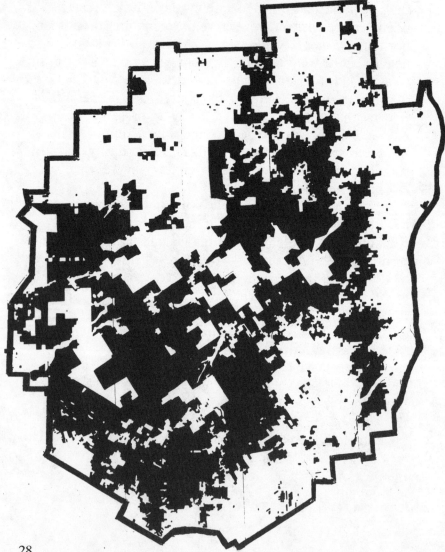

5 - Lampson Falls

The walk to Lampson Falls in the northwestern Adirondacks is so short that you will want to extend it by walking along the trails that lead downstream below the falls. These trails pass a series of smaller waterfalls that are quite beautiful.

From the trailhead, walk west for 0.5 mile to the falls, then turn north along the shore on a trail marked with yellow canoe-carry disks and red markers. The trail is close to the shore and 0.8 mile from Lampson Falls, the trail crosses to the west bank of the river. If you turn left, you can walk back upriver to the falls again.

There is a bluff covered with tall white pine trees beside the falls which makes a lovely picnic spot. Those towering pines are among our biggest evergreen trees and the only one with needles in bundles of five. Look around for the long, slender cones, which also help identify pine trees.

If you turn right, you follow the river downstream beside the series of waterfalls for another 0.8 mile. Where the trail begins to pull away from the river, turn around and head back. If you walk both ways on the west side of the river and return to the falls you will have walked 4.8 miles.

Poison ivy is about the only poisonous plant you have to watch out for in the Adirondacks and there are not too many places where poison ivy grows near trails. One of those places is north of Lampson Falls, just before you reach the bridge. Can you recognize poison ivy? It is easy to stay away from it if you know what it looks like.

If you add the mile round trip to the falls, you will walk a total of 5.8 miles. It is such easy walking you might not even notice the distance.

How long did it take you to walk the Grass River trails? If you only walked a part of the trails, can you figure out how far you walked and how long it took you. Then, can you figure out how fast you were walking?

If I walk on fairly level ground, I can easily walk two miles an hour. I barely walked that fast along the Grass River because there was so much to see and so many places to stop.

Later, the trail descriptions in this book will tell you the **mileage** or how far you will walk and about how long it will take you. This is so you can allow enough **time** to complete your hike during daylight.

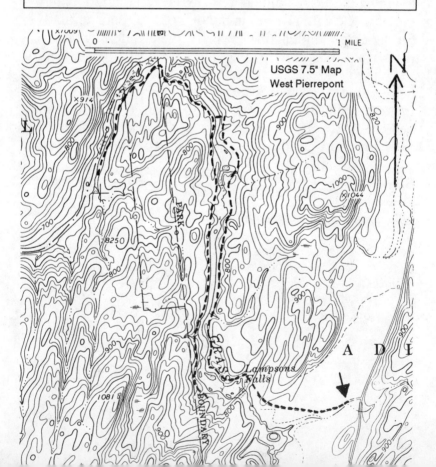

USGS 7.5" Map
West Pierrepont

1 MILE

6 - Auger Falls

Auger Falls is a long series of small waterfalls in a deep gorge on the Sacandaga River, in the southern Adirondacks. There are two routes to the falls. One is a trail marked with official yellow disks and the other is hardly marked at all and then only with red ribbons and unofficial red disks. Either way to reach the gorge takes only ten or fifteen minutes, so you might want to see if you can follow the unmarked route, which we will call a path. A **path** can be followed because the feet of other hikers have worn a **footpath** that you can see. Sometimes there are markers, but only the DEC can mark trails on public land.

The road leads from NY 30 to a cleared area where you can park. Just before the cleared area, another dirt road turns right, south, and parallels the highway. The beginning of the trail is near the south end of this road.

The footpath begins at the edge of the parking area, not far from where the second dirt road turns south. If you feel like exploring it, start walking east. You wind through a stand of tall evergreens, most of which are hemlock trees. You can recognize hemlock by its short needles that are white on the underside. The branches have a lacy appearance and are soft to touch. Hemlocks have very small cones, less than an inch long.

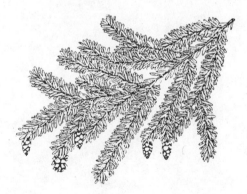

hemlock

The path winds and curves around beneath the hemlocks-it does not follow a straight line like some trails do. Very quickly you will begin to the hear the roar of the falls. When you reach the gorge above the falls, turn south until you see a yellow marker. That is the beginning of the trail that will take you back to the dirt road.

Do not try to climb down to the falls or the river here. The banks are very steep and the hemlock needles that cover the rocks make them very slippery. This is a dangerous place, if you are not careful.

There is a sign near the end of the trail warning you to be careful and to stay up on the slopes above the falls.

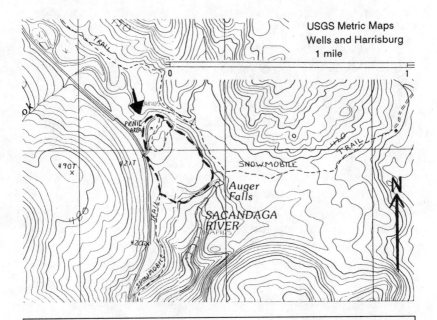

Dangerous places can be found along many of the trails in the Adirondacks. This does not mean that you cannot go there, you just have to know what is safe and proper behavior. Some of the best places to visit in the Adirondacks are among the most dangerous-cliff tops with magnificent views, slippery gorges like Auger Falls, streams you have to cross without a bridge.

You have to be responsible for your own safety and concerned for the safety of those who are hiking with you. Even if hikers obey all the safety rules, accidents can happen. That is why you never hike alone. There are people who can assist you if you are injured, but the best way is to prevent injuries.

If you were to make up safety rules, what would you include? What would you tell someone who was going to Auger Falls?

Be careful near cliffs and lookouts.

Stay on the paths and trails.

Don't jump from rock to rock or from ledges-they can be slippery.

Obey signs that caution you about dangerous places.

Be alert and watch where you are putting your feet.

Don't show-off; someone less agile than you are might try to imitate you.

7 - Jimmy Creek Waterfalls

Not all the best places to visit in the Adirondacks have trails or even paths leading to them. Sometimes you do not need a path. Sometimes you can follow a stream or the shore of a lake and that is the easiest way to get to places without a trail. My favorite place without a trail is another beautiful waterfall and the creek below the falls is filled with a jumble of rocks and boulders.

The falls are located in the southern Adirondacks on a creek that is a tributary of the West Branch of the Sacandaga River. (A place like this where the creek flows into the river is called the **confluence**.)

On the right, east side of Jimmy Creek there is a path that begins to follow the creek upstream, but the path soon disappears. You can walk beside the creek, or in low water right at its edge. The hike to the falls is about a mile long, but you are going uphill all the way. It is harder to walk where there is no trail or path and it takes longer. You may need almost an hour to get to the falls. You will not get lost if you follow the creek, but it is not as easy walking here as it would be if you had a trail to follow.

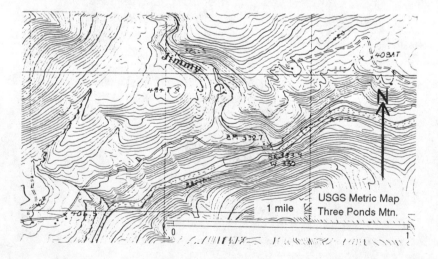

USGS Metric Map
Three Ponds Mtn.

1 mile

0   1

The map we use to show Jimmy Creek is not a sketch map. It is a copy of a map from the **United States Geological Survey**. Can you find West River Road? the West Branch of the Sacandaga River? Jimmy Creek? Which way does Jimmy Creek flow?

The line drawn on the bottom of the map shows how long a mile is on this map. We say it gives the **scale** of the map. Can you estimate how far you have to walk to reach the falls if you follow the creek?

Notice all the curved lines that fill in the map. These are **contour lines**. Each line traces points that are at the same **elevation** or height above sea level. The letters BM stand for Bench Mark; it is a place where the elevation has been measured by the Geological Survey. The number by the letters BM tells the elevation of that point.

The spaces between lines show a difference of 10 meters in elevation change. That is about 30 feet. What is the elevation of the confluence of Jimmy Creek and the West Branch of the Sacandaga? What is the elevation of the waterfalls? Subtracting the numbers gives you the change in elevation, or the vertical distance you have to climb to reach the falls. How much is it in meters? Can you give the figure in feet?

White pine grows taller in the Adirondacks than any other tree.

Other Waterfall Hikes

Shingle Mills Falls on Otter Creek is a short walk in the western Adirondacks. You get to it by turning off NY 12, north of Lyons Falls on Burdicks Crossing Road. Turn off Brantingham Road on to Partridge Road and follow it for 2.6 miles to the dirt road which will take you north to Shingle Mills Falls.

Gleasman's Falls is also in the western Adirondacks. It lies on the Independence River and the trail leading to it is just over 2 miles long. You will need more than an hour to reach the falls, and another half hour or more to follow the trail that stays on the cliff tops above the falls. The falls is a series of cascades that cover nearly half a mile. Finding the trailhead is not easy, so consult the atlas.

Shelving Rock Falls is in the eastern Adirondacks, on the east side of Lake George. A loop trail from Shelving Rock Road leads past the falls. Stay on the trail, because this is another place where the area around the falls can be dangerous. Consult *Discover the Eastern Adirondacks* for directions to the trail.

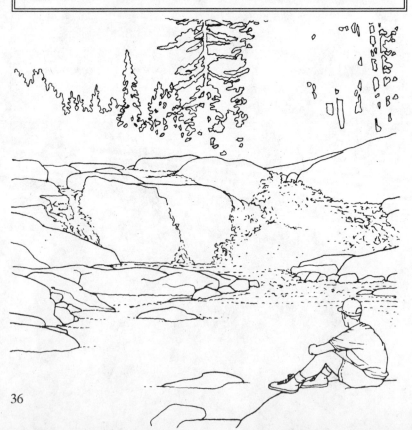

III - Fire Towers

The private lands in the Adirondack Park have always been a source of trees for lumber for the State. About a hundred years ago, just about the time the Adirondack Park was established, lumbermen were careless in the way they left the branches from trees they had cut. At the same time, there was a drought in the Adirondacks. In addition, a railroad was finally completed through the middle of the Adirondack Park and its engines burned logs and coal and sent sparks into the air. The combination of these three things resulted in a number of huge forest fires that raged through the Adirondacks.

To save the forests, the Conservation Department began building tall towers on the tops of some of the mountains. From these towers, fire observers could see and report fires before they got too large.

The fire observers had to reach their cabins and the towers by hiking trails up the mountains. Gradually the forest has recovered from the days of heavy logging. The forest has grown back to protect the water resources. Today's forests rarely burn, and most of the 60 fire towers have been closed because they are no longer needed. One or two are still manned with people who can give you information about the area. Some towers are in such poor condition that the DEC has removed the lower stairs or put chains across them. **Do not climb these towers.**

However, the trails are still there and you can enjoy the views from some of the mountains without climbing their towers. A few of the mountains have towers that you can climb, with care, and Kane Mountain is one of them.

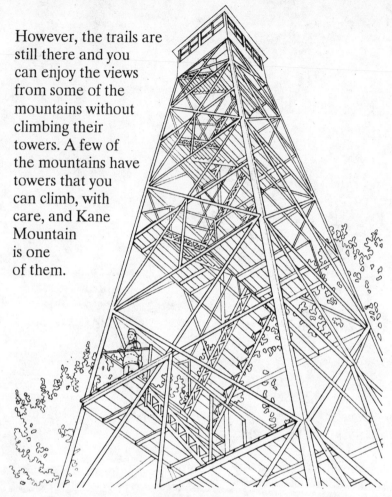

For many years, hikers used to travel around the Adirondacks and climb every tower. The observer would give the hiker a card that told which mountain the hiker had climbed. It is no longer possible to see the whole Adirondacks by climbing fire tower mountains, but mountains with fire towers offer the best climbs for getting acquainted with the Park.

Only two are described in detail, but the list of other fire tower mountains is quite long. Their trails are pretty easy to follow and their trailheads are usually well-marked.

8 - Kane Mountain

Kane Mountain is one of the smaller fire tower mountains. Its location in the very southern Adirondacks makes it easy to get to for many hikers. It is small enough to make it a best choice for a first mountain climb.

There are three trails to Kane Mountain and two are shown on the map. You will use the one that starts near Green Lake.

Opposite the parking area is a guideboard marking the trailhead. This guideboard tells the name of the mountain and the elevation of its summit (2180 feet). The map shows the elevation of Green Lake. Can you figure out how much higher the mountain is than the lake? (Hint: the elevation of Green Lake is about 1450 feet.) That 730 feet difference is what you will have to climb vertically in about 0.8 mile. (The guideboard says the trail is 0.5 miles long; not all Adirondack guideboards give correct information.)

That makes it a good climb, but not a very steep one. You may need forty minutes to reach the tower, but the trail is so wide and easy to follow, you do not need any further description of it.

The southern trail, the one that starts from Schoolhouse Road, is really steep. Maybe you will have time to climb both and see which one you prefer. Maybe sometime you can climb up one trail and down the other.

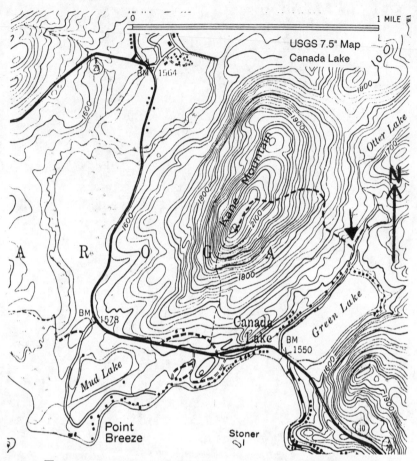

Trees cover the top of the mountain, and you need to climb the tower to see the view. You can look down at Canada Lake and West Lake and on a clear day see peaks south of the Mohawk Valley. Before you climb the tower, think about doing it safely. Hold on with both hands and move one foot or one hand at a time. Don't let anyone you are with fool around on the stairs or in the tower itself. Most of the standing towers have been vandalized. Do not do anything to harm them further.

When you plan to climb a mountain, you can estimate the distance you will have to climb by counting the **contour lines** on the map. On the maps reproduced in this guide, each contour line represents 10 meters or about 30 feet. Notice how the contour lines curve around the mountain, getting smaller and smaller until they reach the summit. Those circles let you know how high you will climb.

(Other maps may have 5-meter intervals between contour lines and some older maps have 20-foot intervals.)

On the map showing some mountains, the contour lines are very close together. This means the mountain is very **steep**. The farther apart the lines are, the less steep the mountain. Some of the slopes of Kane Mountain are very steep. Can you tell which is the steepest side? Of the two trails that are shown, which one is the least steep?

If you climb 100 feet for every 0.1 mile you walk horizontally, then I think the mountain is steep.

9 - Goodnow Mountain

Goodnow Mountain is unusual in that the land around it is privately owned, but the trail and tower are open to the public. Because the mountain is owned by the SUNY Syracuse School of Environmental Science and Forestry, students use the trail to learn how to care for a trail. As a result, the trail is in very good condition.

The well-marked trail makes a moderate climb up 1030 feet in 1.7 miles. It begins on a newly opened section that heads south from the trailhead on NY 28N and starts to climb fairly steeply. After that first, short rise, the trail turns southwest and traverses gradually up the hillside. There are chains of log stringers and numerous bridges over small streams, but the grade is gentle enough so that erosion should not be a problem.

Almost half way to the summit, after a forty-minute walk, you reach a T intersection. Turn left, east, and continue uphill on the old trail.

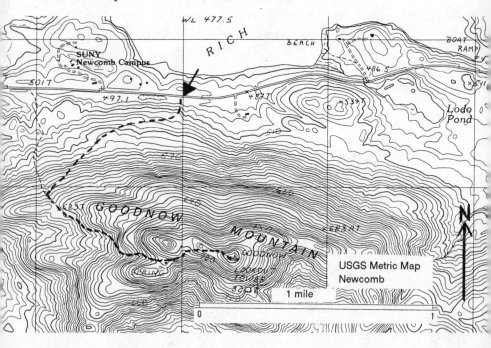

USGS Metric Map
Newcomb

1 mile

A long, curving boardwalk leads past an old foundation, near where there are views to the west. Just beyond, a path forks right from the trail and leads to an old well house that once served the fire observer. The way right leads past the fire observer's cabin and on up the narrow summit ridge. You reach the tower after an hour and a quarter hike. The fire tower has been restored. It even has the large circular map that fire observers used to locate fires. You can use it to help identify the High Peaks you see to the north. Spread out is a panorama of the highest mountains in the Adirondacks. Santanoni, the tallest peak on the left, has a distinctive slash of open rock. The sharp cliffs on Wallface gave that mountain its name. Next to the right is MacIntyre and on to the right is Colden. Marcy, the tallest peak in New York State, is almost hidden behind Skylight.

The Forest Preserve is **public land**, owned by the State government. It is open to anybody-that means you can walk anywhere in the Forest Preserve that you choose to go. As you drive along the highways in the Park, you often see the blue and green disk that represents the Department of Environmental Conservation. This means the land is public and you can walk there.

A bit more than half of the Adirondack Park is **private land**, owned by companies or individual people. Perhaps your parents or friends own land in the Park. Private landowners have the right to post their land with signs that tell the public that there is no public access. This means hikers cannot trespass or walk on the land. There are exceptions. Some private landowners do not post their land and they do let hikers use trails on their land. Sometimes hikers are given permission to walk on trails on private land as they are here. Remember to respect the rights of private landowners who do give permission to hikers to cross their land. And do not trespass where land is **posted**.

Other Fire Tower Mountains

You can find a fire tower mountain in almost every corner of the Park. Some of them still have towers; a few have no towers, but the summits are bare so you do not need a tower to enjoy the view. The towers on this list are all described in *Fifty Hikes in the Adirondacks.* Some of them have short trails, some are very long. The list gives the distance, the vertical rise, and a brief description of how to get to the trailheads.

Bald/Rondaxe is a small mountain with great views over the Fulton Chain Lakes. The trailhead is off Rondaxe Road, a north turn 4.6 miles east of Old Forge. The 400-foot climb is less than a mile long.

Cathead Mountain has a fairly steep trail that rises 1,100 feet in 1.2 miles, but the climb is straight forward and quite easy. Take the Bleeker Road north of Northville and turn onto North Road to the trailhead.

Hadley Mountain has a 2-mile long trail that rises 1,550 feet. The trailhead is on Tower Road, which forks from Hadley Road, northwest of Hadley and Luzerne.

Blue Mountain is very popular. The trailhead is north of the Adirondack Museum. The 2-mile trail rises 1,560 feet and can be climbed in half a day.

Snowy Mountain is the tallest mountain in the southern Adirondacks. You may want to wait to make the 2,100-foot climb until you have experienced other mountains. The trailhead is a parking turnout on NY 30, 17 miles north of Speculator. The 7.5-mile round trip takes 6 hours. The last part of the trail is very steep. The summit is only partly exposed, but the tower should not be climbed.

Owls Head Mountain has a 3.6 mile trail, but it rises only 1060 feet above Long Lake. The trailhead is on Endion Road, the first left turn north of the bridge in the village of Long Lake.

St.Regis Mountain is in the northern Adirondacks, not far from the Paul Smiths Visitors Interpretive Center. Go 2.5 miles west of Paul Smiths College where signs direct you south on a narrow road to the trailhead. The trail is 3 miles long and rises 1,235 feet.

Poke-o-moonshine is in the northern Adirondacks. The trailhead is on NY 9, 3 miles south of Northway Exit 33. The trail climbs very steeply behind the cliff-faced mountain, rising 1,260 feet in a mile.

IV - Ponds and Lakes

The 2,759 lakes and ponds in the Adirondacks come in all sizes and shapes and they are all quite different. Some are so big you need a boat or canoe to explore their shorelines. Some have sandy beaches for swimming, while others have muddy shores with dark brown water.

There are undoubtedly more hills and mountains in the Adirondacks than there are lakes and ponds, but it is an unusual fact that such a large proportion of the lakes and ponds have trails leading to them, while many of the hills and mountains remain trailless. Eight trails to ponds and lakes are described in this chapter, four more are listed as alternates. This selection barely begins to suggest the wonderful diversity of adventures you can find on the shores of Adirondack waters.

10 - Bass Lake

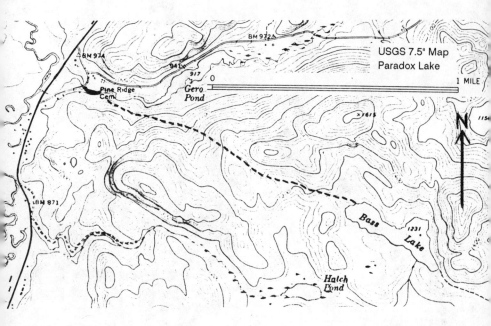

The trail to Bass Lake follows an old logging road that is 1.6 miles long and rises 400 feet between the trailhead and the lake. You can walk it in under an hour, which leaves a lot of time for exploring the lake shore.

The access road ends at the site of an old bridge over Black Brook, but before it ends, you will see the yellow marks that identify the trail heading east to Bass Lake.

The trail briefly follows Black Brook, then begins to climb through a deep woods of hemlocks. Notice how the trees are big and tall and straight. Their size is remarkable because these forests were almost all cut over a century ago so that their bark could be used to tan leather.

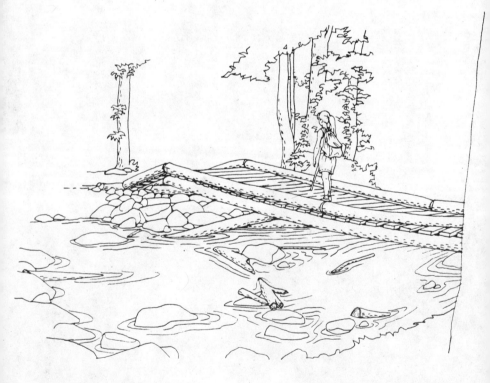

There were two tanneries near North Hudson that made shoe leather from hides brought here from South America and tannin from local hemlock bark.

The trail cuts diagonally across the slope, finding the easiest way up the hillside. The long traverse ends a mile from the beginning. Then the trail winds for nearly half a mile on a level between two hills. Such a level area is sometimes called a draw. Here you will find some truly big hemlocks.

At 1.5 miles, you can spot the lake through the trees. The trail descends to a rock ledge near an inlet of the lake. If you cross the inlet, you can find other ledges and the tops of small cliffs to explore.

The yellow trail continues along the southern shore of the lake, but far back from the shore. If you have time, you might want to follow it to the outlet for more views of cliffs before you return.

Keeping trails open for hikers takes a lot of money and a lot of work by many people. Some trails are maintained by volunteers-someday you may want to volunteer to work on trails in the Adirondacks. Other trails are maintained by the Department of Environmental Conservation. **Trail work** takes many forms: clearing trees that fall down (blowdown); building bridges over streams; placing stones or strings of boards on muddy trails so hikers will stay on the trails; and constructing waterbars. **Waterbars** divert water to the side of the trail so it cannot run down the trail.

The trail to Bass Pond is an example of good trail work. Notice the chains of rocks that keep your feet out of the mud. Notice how the waterbars are built of large stones so they will last. The biggest problem with Adirondack trails is the fact that water likes to follow them, changing trails into streambeds. This will not happen here.

11 - Mitchell Ponds

The trail to Mitchell Ponds is short, but the drive along the road through the Moose River Plains to reach the trailhead is long. However, it is a road full of surprises with many lakes and ponds along it, so if you are camping near Inlet in the west or Indian Lake on the east, you can explore the road while you are heading to Mitchell Ponds. The trailhead is a gated road forking from the main road through the Moose River Plains.

The trail follows an old roadway, and it is relatively level, so the 2-mile walk to the pond will take not much more than an hour. On the way, look for unusual ferns beside the trail. The trail reaches a meadow and forks right. Walk straight ahead to reach a picnic site at the eastern edge of the first pond. From here you have views of the cliffs on the small hill that borders the northern side of the ponds. If you have time, come back and follow the yellow trail from the meadow to a bridge. Just beyond the bridge, the

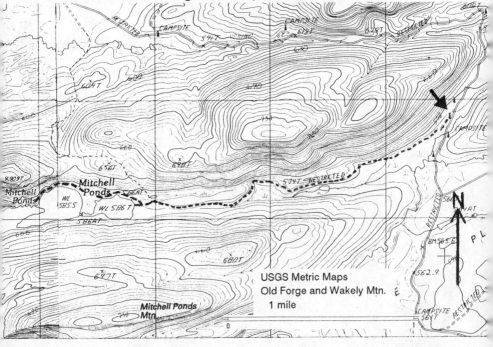

USGS Metric Maps
Old Forge and Wakely Mtn.

1 mile

roadway with the snowmobile trail heads right and uphill. A narrow, yellow-marked trail stays left along the shore of the ponds. You can walk to the far end of the western pond or explore the peninsula that separates the ponds.

The Adirondacks has a number of long **dirt roads**. Some, like the Moose River Plains Road can be driven. Others, like the trail to Mitchell Ponds, have been turned into hiking or snowmobile trails. They have barriers to prevent people from driving trucks, motorcycles, or all-terrain vehicles on them.

12 - Kibby Pond

Kibby Pond is a favorite with fishermen and campers. The trail is nice and short and easy to follow for a day hike.

A guideboard on the north side of the road marks the beginning of a side road. Park on it; the yellow-marked Kibby Pond Trail begins from the roadway, about 100 feet from the highway. The trail heads east across a small stream then swings southeast and climbs 300 feet up the hillside and into a small draw. The trail is level for a short while, then climbs again as it curves around to the east again and crosses a knoll before descending to the pond.

The pond is 570 feet above the road, so you will climb as much to reach the pond as you might to some of the smaller Adirondack hills. You can walk paths along the shore of the pond; there are some pretty spots for a picnic or for camping. If you do plan to hike away from the end of the trail, look carefully at the place the trail reaches the lake so you can find the end of the trail when it is time to return. The trail is just over a mile long, but with the climb, you need to allow nearly an hour to reach the pond.

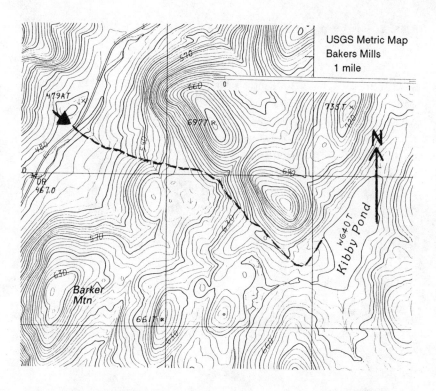

USGS Metric Map
Bakers Mills
1 mile

Kibby Pond

Barker Mtn

Many Adirondack ponds have traditionally had good fishing, but several things have happened to spoil the fishing in a lot of them. Careless fishermen have used live minnows or other fish as bait. These have escaped and thrived and taken the food supply from the native fish. Acid rain has made some ponds so acidic that no fish can live in them.

The Department of Environmental Conservation has programs to stock lakes with native trout and bass. The DEC has added lime to acidic lakes where that is practical. Lime counters the acid levels and makes the water neutral so fish can survive. The DEC has used the chemical rotenone to kill junk fish so the lakes can be restocked with native species. As a general rule, the lakes in the eastern Adirondacks are not as affected by acid rain as those in the western Adirondacks. Kibby Pond has been stocked to improve the fishing.

13 - Grassy and Wilson Ponds

The 2.9-mile trail to Wilson Pond passes Grassy Pond on the way. This trail crosses two small streams that beaver regularly flood and there is no bridge. Walk this way only in low water-the dry times of summer.

The first part of the trail south of the trailhead crosses private land-a path leads from the red-marked trail through the private land, so do not follow it. Stay on the red trail and in just a few minutes you will begin to see the marshes that surround Grassy Pond off to the east. In a little more than ten minutes, about 0.5 mile, look for a side path to the left that leads to the shores of this wet pond.

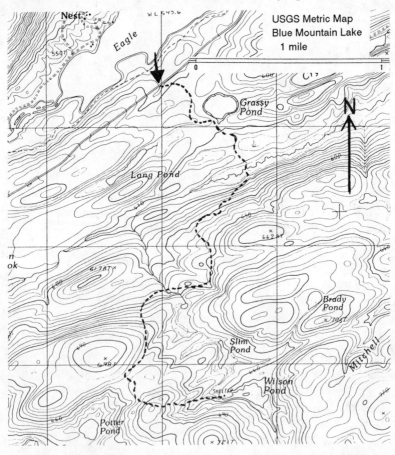

Beavers flood streams to create the ponds they need to live through the winter. Beaver cut trees around the edges of wetlands to make their dams and houses and to store branches for winter food. Without beaver, the woods would become uniformly dense. When beaver leave their ponds, their dams gradually give way, and the ponds dry out, leaving marshes and meadows that attract deer and other animals. Trees spring up in the marshes and fill them in until the next time a beaver decides to build a dam.

Beavers have always made things difficult for hikers. Their ponds flood out many trails and some trails have had to be permanently rerouted. The long chain of marshes on the stream beyond Grassy Pond has been regularly flooded by beaver. The place the trail crosses the stream has always been a problem, but sometimes beaver leave a dry dam that can serve as a bridge across small streams.

If you encounter **beaver flooding** on a trail, you can walk around the edges, looking for the trail again. It might happen that you would have to give up your planned trip and wait until another day.

Back on the red trail, you find logs to help you cross the outlet of Grassy Pond. The trail, which generally heads south, winds about to avoid the marshes. First it heads southeast to cross the outlet of Long Pond-you may find a beaver dam to help you here. Then the trail swings southwest toward more marshes that surround the outlet of Wilson Pond. This point, 0.9 miles from the start, is where you may even get your feet wet. Across the marsh you can see the hill you will climb to reach Wilson Pond. If you can cross the outlet stream-sometimes you can find a well-placed log to help you here-you will see a sign to a spring to the left as you reenter the woods.

At this point, turn right and shortly begin to climb the hill. The trail makes a long traverse that takes you up 260 feet in elevation in a little over half a mile. Then the trail becomes more level and continues winding generally south around several small knolls. Then the trail crosses the outlet of Wilson Pond again.

The outlet of Wilson Pond flows through another series of marshes just after it leaves Wilson Pond. A widening in the outlet is called Slim Pond. The next section of trail is an arc to the west and back that avoids these marshes. The trail crosses several knolls and rocky ridges on the way. This mile-long arc really winds about and up and down and adds considerably to the time it takes to hike to Wilson Pond. It does, however, keep you away from the marshes and Slim Pond.

The trail approaches Wilson Pond from the west. Before it gets there it crosses an intermittent stream (that is a stream that may dry up in summer) and the outlet again. Then it weaves across a bluff for a quarter of a mile. The trail ends at a lean-to near the shore of Wilson Pond. (Lean-tos are open-faced log shelters used by campers.) Picnic here or just beyond on the shore of the pond itself.

14 - Rock and Long Ponds

Rock and Long ponds lie deep in the Siamese Ponds Wilderness north of Speculator. Another long, dirt road leads to the trailhead for the ponds, but this one crosses private land. East Road is open to the public but if you want to do anything on the private land before you reach state land and the public trailhead, you need a permit from the owner, International Paper Company. There is no public camping on this private land.

From the trailhead at the end of East Road, it is 2.5 miles to Rock Pond, another mile to Long Pond, so you can make your hike as long as you want. You can easily walk the 3.5 miles to Rock Pond in under two hours, but you may need more than an hour to drive to the trailhead from Speculator, so plan your day accordingly.

The trail follows an old logging road all the way to Long Pond. The first mile crosses several reforestation areas, places where trees were planted years ago to recover the forests stripped by loggers before 1900. At a mile, a trail forks right, stay left or straight. The trail winds through deep forests, over humps and ridges, but the route is generally level. At 2.5 miles, the trail dips to cross the outlet of Rock Pond. Just beyond a path forks left up the slopes to the ledges above the pond. Swimming in the clear water is especially fine.

For Long Pond, stay straight on the trail-there are few markers, but the way, still along the old roadway, is obvious, except in an area just south of the pond where trees are crowding the trail and making it less easy to spot. The mile-long trail heads east of north from Rock Pond and continues as an unmarked path on the pond's western shore. Follow that path, staying close to shore, to a small rocky peninsula that makes a good picnic spot, with views of the cliffs on Long Pond Mountain across the water.

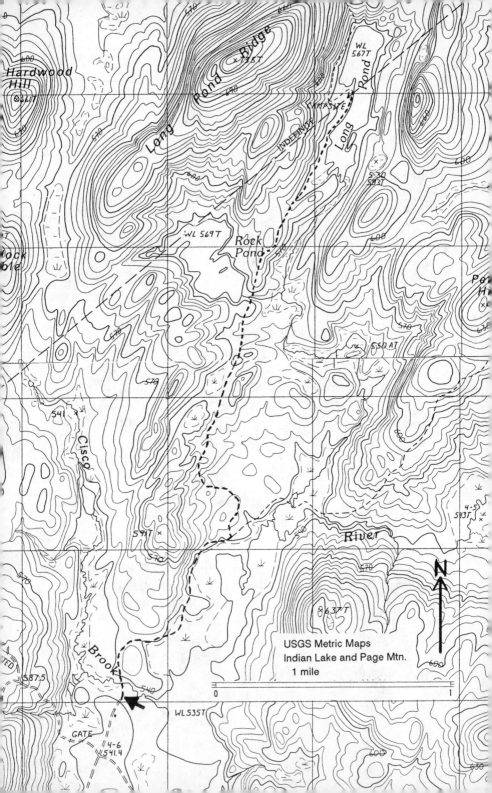

Hardwood
Hill

Long Pond Ridge

WL 567T

Long Pond

INDEFINITE

PASSABLE

WL 569T

Rock Pond

WL 550 AT

Cisco

Brook

River

N

USGS Metric Maps
Indian Lake and Page Mtn.
1 mile

0   1

WL 535T

GATE

In the Adirondack Park, the patches of public land that make up the Forest Preserve are divided into several classifications. The most protected classification is **Wilderness**. Wilderness trails often receive less maintenance than do the trails in the other large classification, **Wild Forests Areas**. In Wild Forests, snowmobiles and sometimes bicycles are permitted on trails that are marked for their use. Wild Forests areas tend to be smaller than Wilderness areas. They usually have more roads leading to and through them. Otherwise the two classifications are very similar.

The trail to Long Pond is in a Wilderness Area. The only difference you might note between the two kinds of trails is that there are fewer markers on Wilderness trails. You will not see many markers on the way to Long Pond. That means you have to be more careful watching for the route, especially if it is filling in with trees and shrubs.

What clues should you look for to keep on the trail? Foot tread, signs of the old road, markers? Will your compass help you here? Notice that you are walking beside marshes as you approach the pond, so these keep you from veering to the east. And, if you are never far from them, you will surely find the pond.

To keep Wilderness areas from being over-crowded, the DEC will limit the number of people in a group of hikers and campers. Wilderness areas are to be managed as quiet places where hikers can get close to nature.

15 - Clockmill Pond

The hike to this pond presents a different kind of challenge. The hike is level and fairly short (1.7 miles), but part of it is not marked. You will need a compass to be sure you are on the right path. Furthermore, the fun of visiting Clockmill Pond is leaving the path to walk along the pond's northern shore, so you have to figure out where the path forks from the snowmobile trail. You also have to notice the end of the path so you will find it for the return.

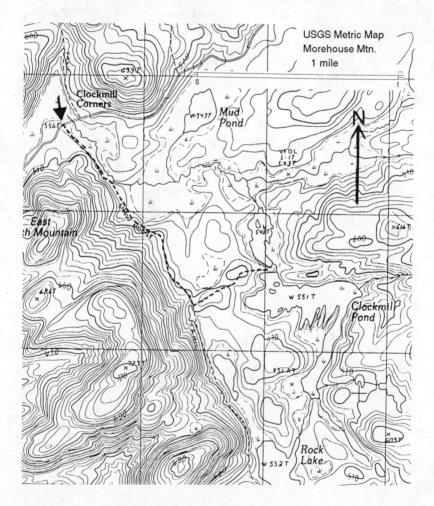

Make sure that you have at least two other friends or relatives along for this trip so you can practice some of the skills you have been learning. First of all, try to **stay in the lead** of your group. That way, you have to watch out for the directions you should take and make decisions on which way to go. If you follow, you will not learn as quickly. But, never get so far ahead you are out of sight of those in your group.

If your group does stray from a trail or path or if the path disappears, stop as soon as you notice that you have lost your way. One of you should stand where you stopped. The others should begin to circle around, always staying within sight or earshot of the one who has stopped, gradually increasing the circles until the trail or path is visible again. This method invariably works, but to use it you must keep your group together at all times.

The Powley-Piseco Road is my favorite dirt road, so you will certainly enjoy the drive to the trailhead. The snowmobile trail begins by heading southeast with marshes visible through the trees off to the north of the trail. The walk is level and obvious as it follows an old road. Just over half an hour into the hike, at 1.2 miles, the trail emerges in a small, open, rectangular meadow. The snowmobile trail cuts straight across the length of the meadow to reenter the woods. An orange snowmobile disk marks the continuing trail.

Shortly after you first enter the meadow, walk to the left and look for an opening in the forest edge that marks another old roadway. This one is unmarked; it heads a little north of east, making a right angle with the snowmobile trail. With some searching about you should find it and with your compass you should be confident you are taking the right direction. Once on the path, you can follow it for the 0.5-mile hike to Clockmill Pond. Note where the path along the old roadway approaches the pond. You will want to get back to this spot for the return. If you are certain you can find it again, walk along the ridge behind the pond's northern shore to the outlet. There is no path so it may take you fifteen minutes to reach the old beaverdam at the outlet. Explore around the dam and just below it you should find a huge toothed wheel-a mysterious object that might mark an old mill, but one that remains mysterious. Why did the pond receive the name Clockmill? Was there a mill? Many mysteries like this surround distant Adirondack lakes and ponds.

For the return, walk back along the shore of the pond to the end of the path, head south of west on the path to the meadow, then north to the trailhead.

16 - Tirrell Pond

Several trails reach Tirrell Pond, and the shortest starts from the same trailhead as the hike to Blue Mountain, at the top of the hill north of the Adirondack Museum on NY 30. The trail begins from the north end of that parking area and it descends 500 feet in 3.25 miles to the pond, so you will be walking uphill for the return. The 6.5-mile round trip may seem like a lot of hiking, but this is a gentle easy trail. Not much more than an hour and a half is required for each leg of the hike. Allow at least two or three hours to spend at the pond. You will find a good sandy beach for swimming and a lean-to and several picnic spots. If you are ambitious, the walk along the pond's southern shore to the outlet is fun. The views across the outlet to the cliffs on Tirrell Pond Mountain are very nice.

The trail begins by heading northeast and is relatively level as it follows an old tote road (a road that was used to carry supplies to lumbercamps or settlements.) After a forty-five minute walk, about 1.6 miles, the trail crosses a stream and then a private road that serves the summit of Blue Mountain. Beyond a second stream, you reach a sign

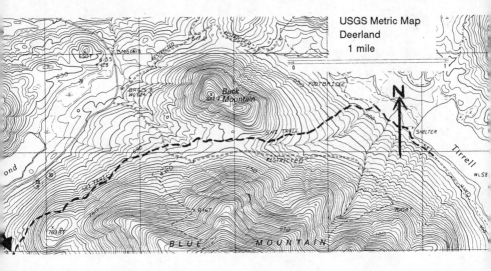

telling you that you are on private land. The trail curves around so it is heading east and begins to descend. It crosses several small streams that drain Blue Mountain and several other old roads. You need to watch for the red markers that will keep you on the correct route.

At 2.8 miles, after the long descent, you reach state land again. The trail crosses a small stream and intersects the blue marked Northville-Placid Trail. Turn right, southeast on that trail for the last 0.5 mile walk to the pond.

Going to the bathroom in the woods: Everyone who hikes should know to do this in a way that will not pollute. If there are **outhouses** along the trail, use them. Outhouses are usually located near lean-tos, but there are not very many of them, and you rarely find one when you need one.

Hikers **find a bush** for privacy, but be sure you pick a spot that is at least 150 feet from the trail and 150 feet from any water. Bury any toilet paper and wastes. Sometimes you can find a stick to dig a small hole, at least 6" deep, but the task is easier if someone in your group carries a small, light weight, plastic **shovel**.

The blue trail continues along the southwestern shore of the pond. If you do not want to follow it, you might want to walk around the shore of the pond to the north.

On the return, start northwest on the blue trail and watch carefully for the fork that takes you back on the red trail. This is another one of those spots where people who are not watching can miss the turn. If you spend more than ten to fifteen minutes on the blue trail after you leave the pond, you have gone too far on it, so turn around and try again to spot the intersection.

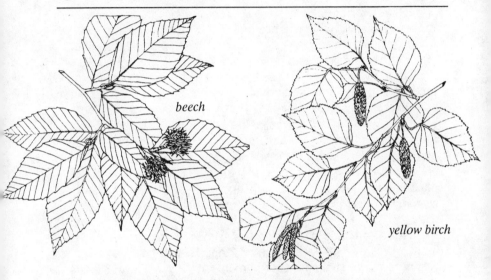

beech

yellow birch

The majority of trees in the Adirondacks are hardwoods and deciduous, that is they loose their leaves in fall. The most common of the dozen or so hardwoods you will see are the maples and yellow birch and beech. Can you tell the difference between yellow birch and beech trees? At first glance their leaves are similar, but they are really quite different. Both have large teeth along the edge of the leaf, but yellow birch has numerous small teeth between each pair of larger ones.

Beech trees have smooth, grey bark on their trunks. Yellow birch has narrow lines on its bark; the bark of mature yellow birch breaks up into plates, but the distinctive lines are still there. Beech have seeds in small round balls, yellow birch have long, thin catkins.

Alternate Pond and Lake Trails

Floodwood Pond is one of the many ponds north of Fish Creek and Rollins Ponds Campgrounds in the northern Adirondacks. The area is laced with a dense network of trails, so you may want to sample several. Drive west on Floodwood Road to the trailhead and hike south to the outlet of the pond.

Gull Lake lies in the southwestern Adirondacks. In Woodgate, turn onto Bear Creek Road from NY 28 and drive to the trailhead at the end of the road. There a large map will help you pick one of two routes to the lake. You may want to combine them into a loop past the lake.

Nine Corner Lake is in the southern Adirondacks. A short, mile-long, trail with snowmobile markers climbs 280 feet to this beautiful lake with its many islands and bays. The trailhead is 200 yards west of the intersection of NY 29 A and NY 10 at Pine Lake. Turn from the snowmobile trail on a path to the outlet or follow the trail along the southern shore.

Newcomb Lake (Santanoni Preserve) is reached by a long (10.2 miles), but very easy walk. The trailhead for Santanoni Preserve is in Newcomb. All of the trail is along a roadway that can only be used by DEC personnel. Take the right fork 2.1 miles from the trailhead. When you reach the lake continue on around the shore to see Camp Santanoni and go past it to find a great swimming beach sheltered by cedars on the northeast corner of the lake.

Hour Pond lies in a Wilderness Area, so expect to find fewer markings along its 4.4-mile path and trail. The trailhead is at the end of Thirteenth Lake Road, south of North River. The trail leads to Old Farm Clearing at 1.2 miles. Turn right on the blue-marked Puffer Pond Trail. The path to Hour Pond forks from this trail at the point the trail crosses Hour Pond Outlet.

V - Hills and Small Mountains

You really have to search to find small hills and mountains with views in the Adirondacks. The best have fire towers and of the rest, few have trails. That is because the trails in the Adirondacks have three basic origins. Of course, trails were built to accommodate the fire towers. Many trails follow old logging or tote roads and these roads were built along valleys or ridges, and they rarely climbed mountains. Most of the actual trail building on mountains has been in the High Peaks region, where the trails are often long and difficult.

There is one more group of mountains with views, those without trails of any sort. These are my favorites, and with experience you can begin to do the kind of hiking needed to reach trailless places. Hiking without a trail is often called **bushwhacking**. For every hill or mountain with a trail, I can think of a dozen or more with no trail, but with an open summit or a cliff top so you can enjoy the rewards of climbing.

For now, lets get more experience hiking to the small hills with trails.

17 - Mount Jo

Everybody's favorite and a great introduction to the High Peaks region is Mount Jo. It starts from the major High Peaks Trailhead at Adirondak Loj at Heart Lake. The trail is marked with numbered stops as a nature trail and there is a pamphlet with information that corresponds to stops on the trail. You can either borrow a copy from the Loj's Nature Center or buy one from the Campers and Hikers Building store.

The trail begins across the road from the lot and shares its beginning with the trail to Indian Pass. Stringers or chains of planks carry you over the wet ground around the Loj for 350 yards to the turn-off for the trail to Mount Jo.

The 2-mile long loop trail leads to the summit, which is 695 feet above Heart Lake. After climbing for 250 yards, the trail splits. The left fork is the longer route to the summit, but it does not matter which way you go as you should plan to make the circuit. Both routes join near the top for the final ascent of the summit, which offers views of Marcy, Colden, MacIntyre, Indian Pass, and Wallface.

You need to allow more than two hours for the climb so you can enjoy the features of the nature trail and learn the names of a few of the High Peaks to the south, places you will want to discover in the future. The huge mountain immediately to the south is MacIntyre, the second highest peak in the Adirondacks.

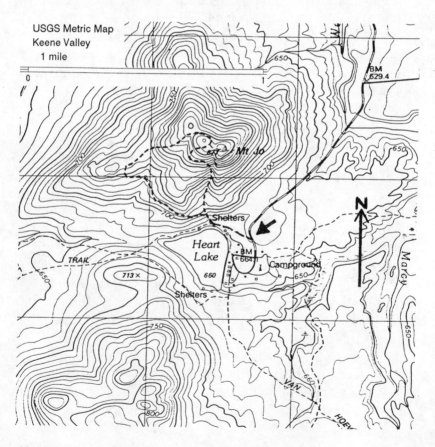

18 - Watch Hill

The trail to Watch Hill is informally marked but it leads to a wonderful short climb with views toward Indian Lake. Park off the highway near where a dirt road heads east. There is no formal parking area. Follow the road as it crosses Griffin Brook and turn north for a ten minute walk to a sign that reads "Pinnacle-Watch Hill." Red squares mark the narrow path that briefly heads east and splits. The left fork is a gentler ascent of the mountain. Stay straight and begin to climb steeply. As the path reaches the ridgeline, the longer trail joins from the north. The path, now quite narrow, winds up and over rock outcrops.

The path dips into a saddle (hikers' term for the dip between two slopes) and climbs to an overlook on a cliff top that overlooks an interior valley. Continue west to the cliff top that overlooks Indian Lake to the south. Three-quarters of an hour is enough for the mile-long, 250-foot climb to the last lookout.

A continuing and not-too-well marked yellow path leads down from it to Indian Lake. If you have time, you might wish to try your skills at path-finding by following the yellow markers. Be sure you note where the path ends at lakeshore-you will need to find this spot to start the return.

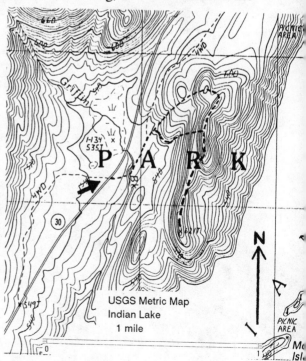

USGS Metric Map
Indian Lake
1 mile

19 - Deer Leap

The Tongue Mountain Range is a long peninsula of
land that thrusts south into Lake George, separated from
the mainland by Northwest Bay. Rugged trails wind over the
summits of the peaks that make up the Tongue-Brown and
Fivemile mountains, Fifth Peak, French Mountain, and First
Peak. Cliffs face the lake side of the Tongue so there are a
number of wonderful places with views. You will want to
come back and hike these trails, but start with Deer Leap,
which is a short introduction to the range.

The 1.6-mile hike to Deer Leap takes you up and
down over several small knobs on the way to the overlook,
which is less than an hour from the highway. The return
walk takes about the same time, though if you explore all

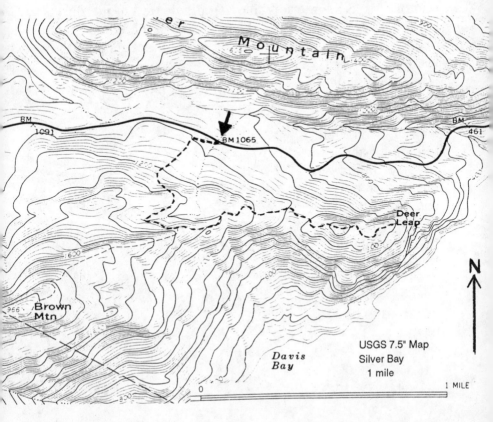

the side paths and view spots, you will need much more than two hours for the round trip.

The trail begins across the road from the parking area and heads west then south from the highway, climbing gradually. There is an outhouse at 0.5 mile and just beyond, at a height-of-land, you reach a trail intersection. The way right heads toward French Mountain. Go left toward Deer Leap on the yellow trail. You leave the tall trees of the Tongue's western slopes and begin to walk through the scrubby oak forests that have seen loggers and fires in the past.

The trail begins to descend. You will notice paths forking from the main trail, leading to overlooks. One, 0.3 mile from the intersection, has yellow markers and you should take it for it leads to the best views of the hike. The main trail descends into a small valley, then climbs to a ridge again where there are more views. Crossing the ridge, you will see more paths leading to overlooks. You descend to another overlook, and the final descent leads to an overlook that may be a disappointment-trees are growing up to conceal Deer Leap's views.

On the return you may want to explore some of the side paths that you missed on the way in. You can look across the lake and south to Black Mountain with its fire tower. Islands dot the Narrows of the lake near the tip of Tongue Mountain. One vantage point allows you to look down the length of the Tongue with its cliffs and peaks.

The sign at the beginning of the trail to Deer Leap warns you to look out for **rattlesnakes**. Only mountains on the shores of Lake George and a couple of isolated peaks in the eastern Adirondacks have the rock formations that attract colonies of rattlesnakes.

The Adirondacks is unique in that no other wild animal or reptile will bother you when you are hiking. Bears may bother you when you go camping, but they are only after food and there are ways to foil them.

Avoiding rattlesnakes is not difficult. First of all, watch where you put your feet. Second, do not reach out to a rock or crevice that you cannot see. Third, listen for the rattle the snakes make. Sometimes in spring or fall, rattlesnakes emerge to sun themselves on exposed rock ledges. For all the hiking I have done and for all the looking I have done, I have yet to find a rattlesnake. If you see one, keep away from it, but do not harm it. Rattlesnakes are rare and the species is protected.

20 - Rocky Mountain

The Adirondack's highest peaks are clustered in the eastern Adirondacks-that is where most of the mountains with views are located. Only a few hills in the western Adirondack foothills have views, and one of the easiest offers a short hike with views of the Fulton Chain. The trail is only 0.5-mile long, but it rises 450 feet above the lake, so the way is relatively steep.

The trail begins from the west end of the huge parking turnout. Yellow and orange disks and painted blazes mark the short trail which is quite eroded and in need of trail work. The trail leads across the rocky summit to several nice picnic places, but the rocks are marred by graffiti.

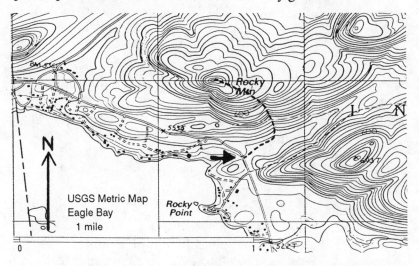

USGS Metric Map
Eagle Bay
1 mile

Grafitti are marks or names painted or scratched on rocks and trees. They destroy the natural beauty. Making such marks in the Adirondacks is against the law. You and your friends would never do that.

21 - Scarface

A longer walk and a bigger climb should help you decide if you are ready for some really big mountains. Scarface is visible from NY 86, east of Lake Placid-it's open rock making an obvious scar on the mountainside. The red-marked trail is 3.2 miles long and climbs 1480 feet. The climb should take two hours, so make sure you have at least four hours to spend on this hike.

Red disks lead you from the trailhead through a pine plantation, across the tracks of the "Fairytale" Railroad that used to run between Remsen and Lake Placid. Sparks from the old steam engines started fires all along the track and the area was replanted with different kinds of pine trees almost a hundred years ago. The trees are tall and straight and beautiful. What clue can you see that tells you that this is not a natural forest, that it was planted?

At 0.5 mile, you cross Ray Brook on a wonderful new bridge. A chain of boardwalk takes you across the swamps that surround the brook. The trail winds through more forests and meadow and back to forest as it heads southwest on a fairly level course.

At 1.5 miles, you reach the old trailhead, which was closed because a prison is located nearby. Turn left along the tote road that was part of the old trail and in five minutes, in another quarter mile, you turn left again off the tote road onto a narrow trail. The trail follows Ray Brook, then leaves the brook and begins to climb, heading southeast, then south. The steady climb takes you through a forest of huge hardwood trees. What ones can you identify? At 3 miles, a steep pitch brings you to the first open ledge, which looks west toward Ampersand and Oseetah Lake. A side path leads to an overlook toward Whiteface Mountain.

A few minutes more on the trail takes you to a second open ledge that looks southeast toward the High Peaks and south toward the Sawtooth Range and the Seward Range.

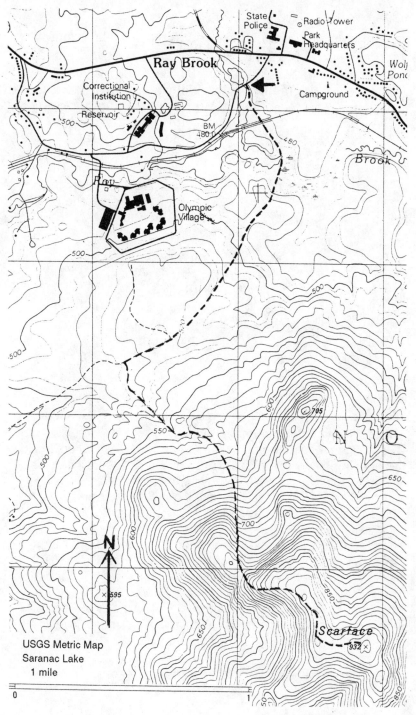

State Police

Radio Tower

Park Headquarters

Ray Brook

Correctional Institution

Reservoir

Campground

BM 480.0

Brook

500

450

450

Ray

Olympic Village

500

500

500

500

500

500

600

705

N O

650

550

650

600

700

N

× 595

600

650

850

Scarface

932 ×

USGS Metric Map
Saranac Lake
1 mile

0   1

Five minutes on the trail takes you to the actual summit, where there is only a small view. The first two overlooks are the best.

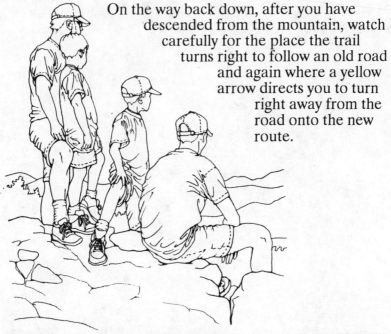

On the way back down, after you have descended from the mountain, watch carefully for the place the trail turns right to follow an old road and again where a yellow arrow directs you to turn right away from the road onto the new route.

Other Hill and Small Mountain Hikes

Gilligan Mountain has a 1.2-mile trail that takes you on a 780-foot climb from the trailhead to an overlook. The trailhead is on the east side of NY 9N, 3.6 miles north of the intersection of routes 73 and 9N, which is just west of exit 30 of the Northway. This easy to follow hike has superb views toward the Dix Mountain Wilderness Area.

Silver Lake Mountain in the northern Adirondacks has cliffs and views and a wonderful, steep trail. The 900-foot climb in 0.9 mile takes under an hour. The trailhead is 1.8 miles north of Taylor Pond Campground on Silver Lake Road.

Echo Cliffs are a part of Panther Mountain, north of Piseco in the southern Adirondacks. The 0.75-mile trail climbs 700 feet from the trailhead, which is 2.6 miles north of NY 8 on Old Piseco Road.

VI- Deep Woods Hikes

Sometimes you will want to hike to a specific destination-like those described in other chapters in this book. Sometimes you may just want to walk through a beautiful forest to enjoy the quiet woods. By setting aside the Forest Preserve, New York State has done a magnificent job of preserving forests.

Most of our forests have been logged at one time or other. One of the deep woods walks below takes you through an area that may never have been cut. The other, with equally tall and beautiful trees, takes you to an area that was logged, but the logging was done a long time ago-about 120 years. Then, nothing but the red spruce and pine were cut for these were the only trees that could be floated to sawmills downstream. The logging was so light that you probably cannot tell the difference between the two forests. Both have large red spruce, tall and straight, the kind of trees that were the most sought after by nineteenth century loggers. You can recognize spruce by the short, stiff, angular needles that are a very dark dull yellowish green. Unlike pine and hemlock trees, spruce trees never have trunks with a very large diameter; a 30" spruce is very big for the species.

Today these spruce shelter a rich understory of plants and they hold enough moisture so the forest floor is almost always damp. Take along a tape measure and try to find the biggest spruce on these walks. Also measure the hemlocks and any pine you might find.

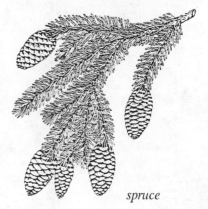

spruce

22 - Fawn Lake

This short walk into a deep forest can be extended in several directions. One of them will give you a bit of practice with map and compass, walking off the trail if you feel you are up to it.

The parking area serves as trailhead for a snowmobile trail that loops through wonderful forests all the way around to the network of ski trails near Piseco Airport. Start out and walk the trail as far as you want, or make one or more detours. The first chance to detour is just 0.2 mile from the trailhead, hardly a five minute walk. A left, unmarked, fork

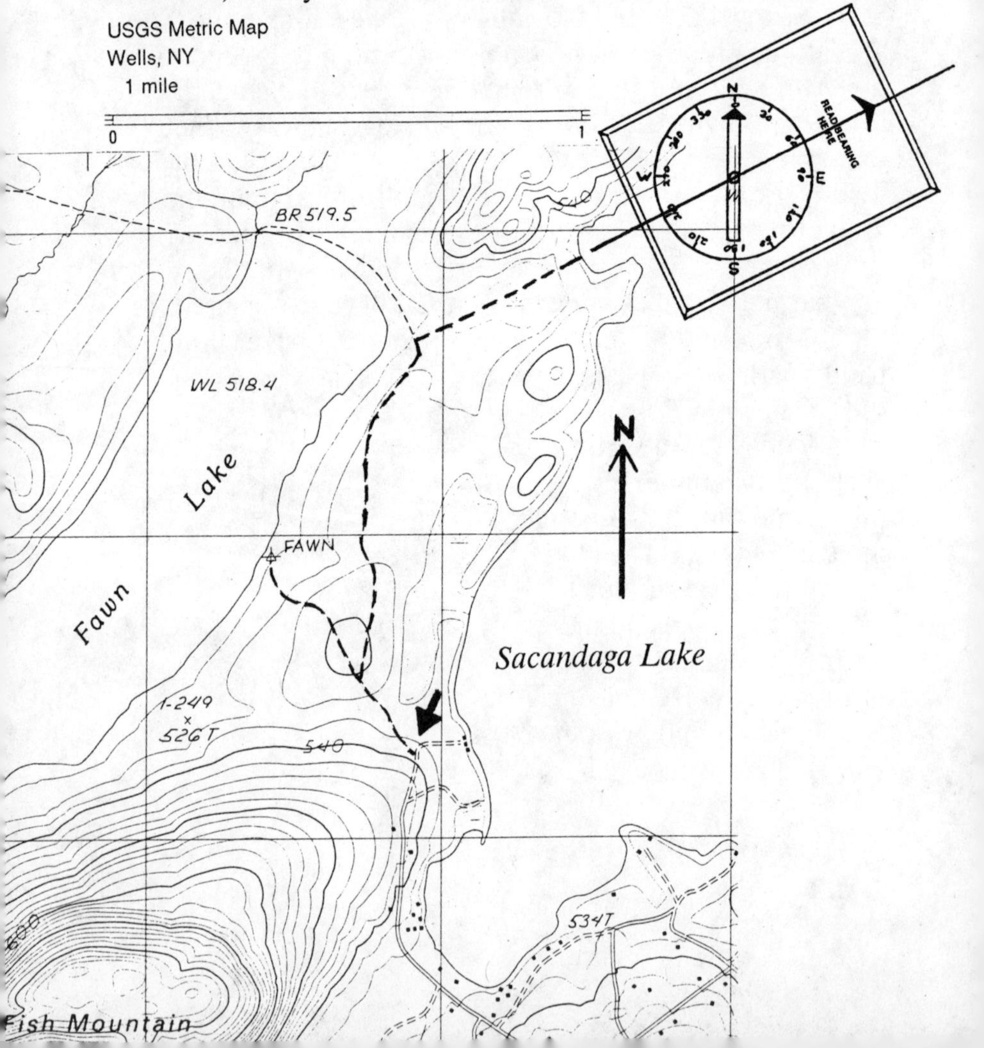

USGS Metric Map
Wells, NY

1 mile

0   1

BR 519.5

WL 518.4

Lake

FAWN

Fawn

λ-249
x
526 T

540

REACH BEARING
HERE

N

Sacandaga Lake

λ-249
x
526 T

534 T

Fish Mountain

takes you to the shore of Fawn Lake where you can find other paths along the lakeshore. The main trail circles around the eastern end of Fawn Lake and reaches planking that carries the trail through a wet area adjacent to the head of the lake.

The short walk, one mile in less than half an hour, to this point is through a forest of huge yellow birch, pines, and maples. At the end of the planking, Fawn Lake is visible through the trees on your left and there is a faint path on your right. Take out your compass and either follow this path or use your compass to show you how to walk the 0.5 mile to the shore of Sacandaga Lake.

USGS maps are oriented toward **true north**, the north pole. Your compass is a circle divided into 360 degrees with north at 0 or 360 degrees. The arrow points toward **magnetic north**, which in the Adirondacks is 14 degrees west of true north.To find the route between the lakes, draw a line on the map showing the route and extend it to the edge of the map. Put your compass where the line intersects the edge of the map and aline the north-south axis of your compass with the edge of the map. The compass indicates the route you want is at 64 degrees. In order to find out the compass or magnetic direction, add 14 degrees to get 78 degrees. You will walk toward 78 degrees as indicated on your compass.

When you want to return you reverse the process. The map and compass tell you you should head toward 244 degrees from true north. Add 14 degrees. Your compass or magnetic heading is 258 degrees.

As you head into the woods spot a tree ahead at 78 degrees magnetic and walk toward it; when you reach it, spot another tree in the same direction. When I am heading out cross country with friends, we spread out about 100 feet apart. The one in the lead charts the route, while those behind check to make sure the leader is following the correct direction.

Using a Map and Compass

Your compass is divided into 360 degrees. The arrow points toward magnetic north, 0 or 360 degrees. You want to be able to compute the **magnetic direction** you want to take. However, the USGS maps you will use are oriented toward true north. Every USGS map has two arrows that indicate the difference between true and magnetic north. In most of the Adirondacks, magnetic north is 14 degrees west of true north. That is why you added 14 degrees to the course you wanted to take to find the magnetic direction.

To review how to find the map direction, first draw a line between the point on the map where you will start and the point you want to get to. Extend that line to the edge of the map, which points to true north. Put you compass on the intersection of the line and the edge of the map. You can read the number of degrees for your course on the map. Now add 14 to get the magnetic direction you should take.

Many adults have trouble making this correction. Find someone who really understands using a compass this way and practice with him or her. You may want to attend one of the workshops in map and compass reading that are offered by different groups. You will need a lot of practice before you can safely find your way with map and compass.

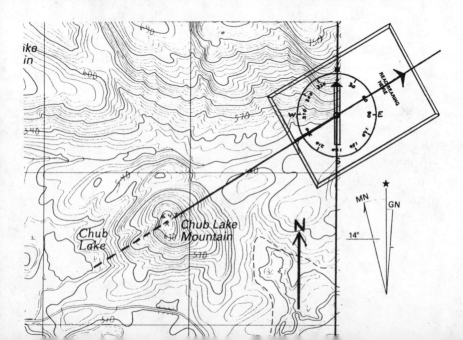

23 - Northville-Placid Trail South of Whitehouse

The Northville-Placid Trail is a long trail that crosses
the Adirondacks from south to north. Parts of it pass
through some of the most beautiful wilderness areas in the
Park. Others are along dusty, dull roads that are open to
vehicles. Hikers choose either to hike the trail in one long
backpacking trip that takes about two weeks or to hike it in
segments that last about a day. One of the most beautiful
stretches is in the Silver Lake Wilderness south of
Whitehouse. Whitehouse was a lodge for hunters and
fishermen on the West Branch of the Sacandaga River.
When the state acquired the lodge and the surrounding
land, the buildings were burned and only the stone chimneys
remain.

Just getting to the trailhead is an adventure.
Sometimes the road just before the parking area is flooded,
so you may have to park 200 yards short of the end and
walk. The trail begins at the west end of the parking area
and heads west for 250 yards to a trail register. The way left
is the trail to Piseco-save it for another day.

Before you turn right, think about how far you might
like to go. This might be a good place for you to see how far
you can walk comfortably in a day. The highest point you
might reach is a draw 700 feet above the river. You can
certainly walk as far as Mud Lake, 2.8 miles to the south and
return. You might even want to continue on to Canary
Pond, which is 6.4 miles from the start. Are you ready for a
12.8-mile hike? Even if you decide it is too much, continue
on for a ways south of Moose Pond, for the forest, which is
everywhere good along this trail, is really wonderful south of
Moose Pond where the trail is in a valley to the east of
Moose Mountain. The trail leads you through deep spruce
forests, up slopes where more and more hardwoods
dominate the forest. This is one of the best woods walks in
the Adirondack Park. Like all parts of the Northville-Placid

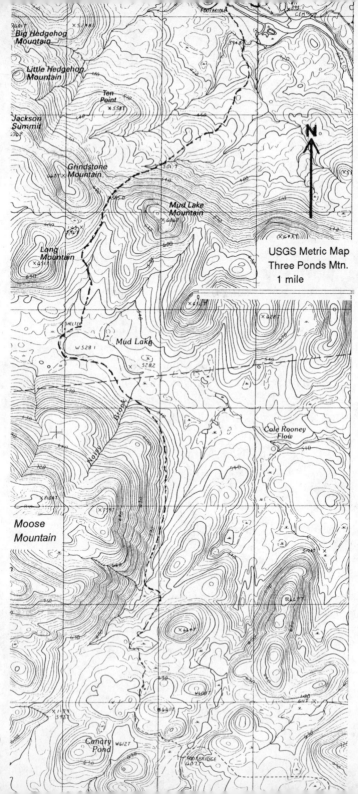

USGS Metric Map
Three Ponds Mtn.
1 mile

Big Hedgehog Mountain

Little Hedgehog Mountain

Ten Point

Jackson Summit

Grindstone Mountain

Mud Lake Mountain

Long Mountain

Mud Lake

Cole Rooney Flow

Moose Mountain

Canary Pond

Trail, this section is well marked with blue disks. Follow the trail south as far as you would like, allowing at least an equal amount of time so you can return to the trailhead.

Start the hike by turning left at the trail register, past a chimney from the lodge and an enormous suspension bridge over the West Branch. On the far side of the bridge, you immediately spot huge spruce trees. They never grow as big as our pines, but some spruce that you will see along this part of the trail are almost as big as they can get.

The trail heads east, crosses a small stream, then turns south, then gradually west of south as it begins to climb the range of hills south of the river. The trail rises gradually as it heads south, though the climbing required is not great. At 1.7 miles, you cross a stream and continue climbing up through a draw. Two miles from the start, you climb into a saddle between two unnamed hills. Then you descend about 200 feet in elevation in about 0.8 mile to Mud Lake, where there is a lean-to.

The trail curves around the west end of Mud Lake, then circles east, crosses Noisey Brook at 3.8 miles, then takes a more southeasterly, then southerly course to round Moose Mountain. There are several small stream crossings, then at 5.2 miles you reach a large beaver dam that once flooded the meadow to the south. The trail now circles around the wet edges of the meadow and climbs back into the forest to rejoin the older trail which had been flooded out. The trail rises slightly as it winds along beside several marshy areas. There is a slight downhill before you reach Canary Pond at 6.4 miles. You have to leave the trail to reach rocks at the shore of the pond where you can enjoy a picnic. This stretch of trail is what hiking is all about-getting away from noise and people, finding out how strong and independent you are. What makes this forest seem so beautiful? Is it the tall trees or the quiet? Few places in the eastern United States have forests any more enjoyable than this.

Hikers understand what their bodies and legs can do, how much **stamina** they have. They know their limits and they do not try to exceed them. If you are not feeling well, you should not hike. If you think you are getting tired, rest for a short while, but cut short your trip. Only you can tell how far you can comfortably hike. Only you will know how far you can climb in a day. Accidents are more likely to happen when you are tired, so it is wise to know your limits. Of course, the more you hike, the stronger you will get, and the farther you will be able to hike.

An Alternate Deep Woods Hike

Pine Orchard on the snowmobile trail northeast of Wells has the most magnificent and accessible stands of pines in the Park. Take Griffin Road north of Wells and turn onto Windfall Road and then turn right at an unmarked fork to a private parking area. The owner permits hikers who respect private property to walk across his land to begin the 2.4 mile walk along the abandoned roadway to Pine Orchard.

VII - Bogs

One of the most unusual places a hiker can explore is a bog and the Adirondacks has a number of bogs. Bogs typically surround bodies of water that have little flow in or out. The water is naturally very acidic. Mats of sphagnum moss grow out from the edges of a bog. These mats can be very thick, even thick enough to support small trees, usually black spruce or tamarack. Tamarack trees are the only ones with needles that fall off in the fall. (We say tamaracks are deciduous.)

Insectivorous plants such as pitcher plants or sundew grow on the sphagnum mats. These unusual plants trap insects and digest them. The mats also support cranberries, orchids, and bladderworts. Shrubs such as myrca gale, leatherleaf, and bog rosemary grow around the edges of a typical bog.

24 - Pitcher Pond

This typical bog lies in the Independence River Wild Forest, where sandy roads and dirt tracks have been turned into a network of horse and hiking trails.

A red-marked trail (the Hiawatha Horse Trail) heads south from the trailhead entrance road to the Otter Creek Horse Trail network, then loops east to intersect a yellow marked trail-called Confusion Flats Road-at 1.4 miles. Follow that road east, then south to a second intersection at

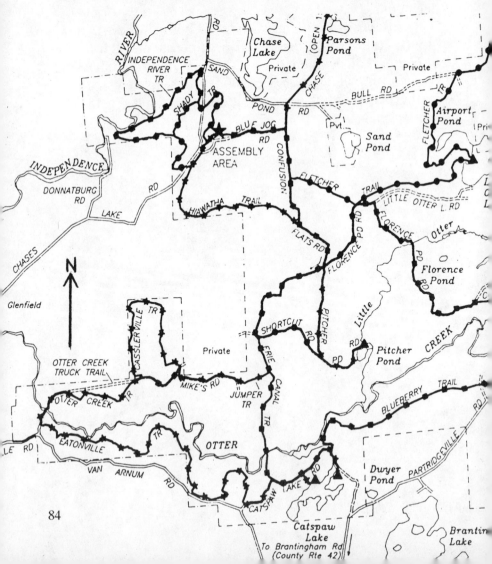

1.9 miles, this one the crossing of Florence Pond Road, which has yellow markers. Pitcher Pond Road is straight ahead, marked with red disks. Alternatively, you can drive west from near the Assembly area on Blue Jog Road, then turn south on Confusion Flats Road to Florence Pond Road. Continue straight on Pitcher Pond Road for 0.6 mile to where it intersects Shortcut Road. Bear left, east, then north for 0.4 mile to Pitcher Pond. A narrow ridge of sand and gravel surrounds the pond. It is called an esker. It was formed by deposits left by a river running beneath the glacier, which once covered this area. The Pitcher Pond Trail and an unmarked path let you make a complete circle around the pond so you can look for its bog plants.

Other Accessible Bogs

Chub Lake lies north of NY 10 in the area the highway takes on an east-west course between the two bridges over the West Branch of the Sacandaga in southern Hamilton County. There is a small path leading to this bog, 200 yards south of the parking turnout that is south of the northern bridge.

Silver Lake Bog, described briefly in the section on nature trails and boardwalks is another bog.

Sunday Pond is a true kettle bog, that is one where a depression was formed by a chunk of ice that remained after the main glacial sheets retreated. The mile-long trail starts from NY 30, 2.1 miles east of Floodwood Road in the northern Adirondacks.

Bloomingdale Bog is north of Saranac Lake and west of Bloomingdale. The raised bed of an old railroad crosses the bog and there is access to the railroad from several roads.

VIII - Big Hikes and Mountain Climbs

Some of the most wonderful hikes in the Adirondacks are long and strenuous, often with quite steep climbs. The trails in this section are more difficult for various reasons. They tend to be in the more rugged northern and eastern Adirondacks or near the High Peaks.

For these longer climbs, you will want to be sure to carry a sweater or jacket, even in summer, so your day pack will definitely get heavier. Rain gear is very important. The weather on the taller summits is cooler and wetter and changes more quickly than in the lowlands.

You will also need sturdy boots with good support. The trails are steeper and rougher. A great deal of the time you will be walking on open rock. Loose rock and rubble and slippery, wet places are everywhere. You need to protect your ankles and you need boots with soles that do not slip.

After you complete these hikes, you should be ready to try some of the Park's tallest peaks. You may even find that you want to try backpacking so you can extend the distance you can walk and climb.

Beneath the title of each of the four trails described in this chapter is a line giving distance, vertical rise, and estimated time for the trip. Most guidebooks summarize this information in just this way. Some add information about sources of maps and color of trail markers. When you start using other guides, don't read this information and think you can go off on the hike without reading the whole text. Guidebooks will tell you what problems you may encounter. They will also tell you to look for interesting things along the trail, things that you might miss otherwise.

Did you notice that a few of the trail descriptions in this guide were very short? The trails are so easy to follow that you need little other information. As you gain more experience, you will find that all you need for most hikes is a map and compass.

Just as a compass tells you what direction you are following, an **altimeter** will tell you approximately how high you are above sea level. Altimeters work by registering changes in atmospheric pressure, so you have to reset them every time you pass a known point such as a bench mark. I find that an altimeter is one of the most useful things in my pack. It tells me how I am doing when I am climbing big peaks and it helps me find cliff tops and rock outcrops where I can enjoy views. If you are serious about climbing, you may want to save up for an altimeter.

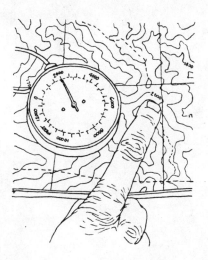

25 - The Crows

Distance - 3.6 mile loop, vertical rise 1,100 feet, time - 3 to 4 hours

Two rocky crags loom above Keene and their summits offer splendid views of the High Peaks to the southwest. It is a 2.4-mile loop over both Big and Little Crow, if you have cars at either end. If not, adding the walk along O'Toole Road makes this about a 3.6-mile loop.

Dark red ADK trail markers identify the trail which begins from the back of the clearing. One of the trails to Hurricane Mountain also begins from this clearing, but guideboards will tell you which way to start.

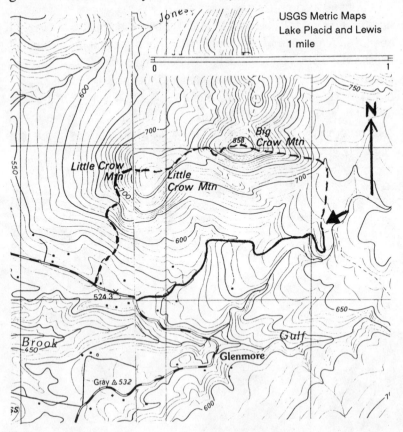

After just a few minutes of hiking, you start to climb and almost immediately you begin to enjoy the views for which the Crows are famous. At 0.5 mile, you reach a fork. Stay left and in another 0.2 mile you reach the summit of Big Crow. Your walk should have taken a little over half an hour to this point. The views are in every direction except to the north. Can you spot Giant? Hurricane? The Dixes?

You can see Little Crow from Big Crow. Cairns (mounds of stones) and paint blazes on bare rock direct you off the bare rock of Big Crow, into the sparse woods, and down into a col (valley) between the two mountains. Little Crow has two summits connected by bare rock, and there are good views from both. From the western summit, a combination of cairns, paint blazes, and markers direct you to a steep, zigzag course down to East Hill Road. Turn left, uphill on East Hill and O'Toole roads to the parking area.

This hike can take as little as two hours, but make sure you have three or more to enjoy the views and puzzle out the mountains to the southwest.

Use your compass to identify distant peaks. If you have a USGS map of the area, you can compute their direction from Big Crow. If not, experiment with identifying Giant at 185 degrees magnetic, Dix at 200, Hurricane at 165, and Cascade and Porter at 250.

26 - Peaked Mountain

*Distance - 8.4 miles, round trip, 1,100-foot vertical rise, time -
5 to 6 hours*

This is a fairly rugged hike that requires you to think
about the route on the way. You will need at least three
hours for each direction, so make sure you have enough
time to complete the trip. Stopping at Peaked Mountain
Pond, after a 3.3-mile, 550-foot climb makes a good hike, if
you decide not to climb the mountain.

From the trailhead near the foot of Thirteenth Lake,
the trail follows quite closely along the western shore of the
lake, sometimes at lake level, sometimes on ledges above
the lake. It will take you a half hour or more to walk the
mile south to the fork to Peaked Mountain Pond. The fork
is not too well marked, but the outlet of the pond flows into
Thirteenth Lake just beyond the fork, so use that as your
guidepost.

It is a very pretty climb along the outlet, up fairly
steeply at first, then more gently. After nearly thirty minutes
and a 0.8-mile hike from the lake, the trail crosses the
outlet-there is no bridge here, so be careful hopping rocks.

The trail continues on the south side of the outlet
stream, which is now fairly level and surrounded by marshes.
Past the first marsh a number of red markers point you to
your right across the stream and into the woods. This loop to
the north takes you around the second marsh and back to
the south side of the brook. Even here, beaver work is
flooding the trail. To the west, over the marsh is your first
view of Peaked Mountain. The trail follows the south side of
this third marsh, winds between some huge boulders, and
heads back into deep woods away from the outlet. This
point, about 2 miles from the lake, is the first of several
confusing spots-it is easy going west, but more difficult to
follow heading east, so observe your surroundings carefully.

The trail stays in the woods until it reaches the outlet of Peaked Pond. It crosses the outlet and circles around the east side of the pond. There are several paths leading to shore so you will have to be alert for markers. On the northern shore, the trail leaves the pond to begin a steep climb up the mountain. Many markers define the trail, which has some very steep sections. Near the top, the trail is quite close to the edge of the cliffs that face the western side of the mountain. Be very careful here. The top of the mountain is a tiny open peak with wonderful views.

On the way down, make sure you can see the next marker at every point on the descent from the mountain.

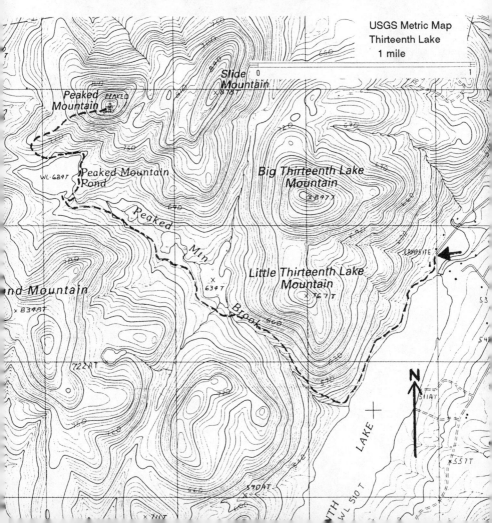

The trail to Peaked Mountain Pond and Peaked Mountain is a **Wilderness trail** and as such it has minimal markings. Hikers have gotten lost and twisted around trying to climb these trails. This is a good time to think about what you should do to avoid getting lost and what to do if you should get off the trail.

First of all, the trail description warns you about several difficult places in the trail, places where you might have trouble. Note these spots carefully as you approach them and observe trees, boulders, streams or other features that mark them. Think about what the trail is doing at these places.

Then, pull out your compass and double check that you are heading in the direction the trail or the guide indicates is proper. Before the trail to the summit of Peaked Mountain was marked, hikers occasionally headed west down from the summit. What direction should you take? The trail around the pond can be confusing because there are several side paths. When you circle the pond, remember that you have to cross the outlet before you will find the trail along the stream for the return.

It is not likely that you will lose the trail on the way out or as you begin to descend from the summit, that is if you have carefully noted the direction you should take. But suppose you cannot find the trail from the shore of the pond. Can you find the outlet? The trail generally follows the outlet back to Thirteenth Lake, although it goes back and forth across the outlet. The outlet is a good route to follow down to the lake. Even if there were no trail, it would lead you to the lake. Heading downstream beside brooks or rivers is one of the best ways to get out if you do lose a trail. Don't follow one unless you have checked the map and are sure that it is headed where you want to go with the shortest route.

Always stay with your companions so you are never alone.

If you really get lost, sit down and think. Do not panic. You have told someone where you were headed, so someone will find you. If you cannot think of a logical way to get out, just sit tight and wait for rescue.

If you take your time and learn how to read a map and understand the forests you are walking in, you will never need rescuing. Hiking, for those who are careful, is really safe.

27 - Treadway

Distance - 10.4 miles, 830-foot vertical rise, time - 5 to 6 hours

This hike in the eastern Adirondacks is along a series of trails with many intersections. Following the segments is good practice for later hikes in the eastern High Peaks, where the trail network is even more complicated.

The trailhead is in the Putnam Pond State Campground. Park in the day use parking area. You can walk either south or north around Putnam Pond to reach the Treadway Trail, but the trip north is 1.5 miles longer. If you go that way, the one-way walk to the mountain is 5.2 miles long with a climb of 830 feet.

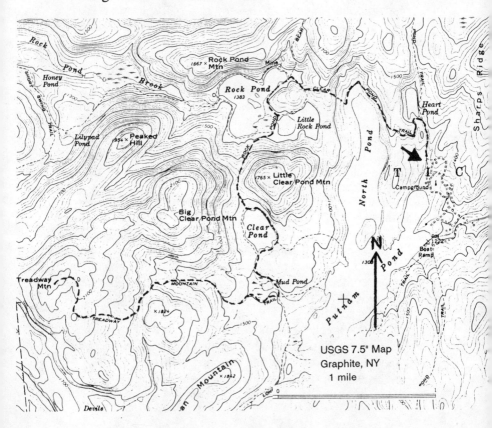

USGS 7.5" Map
Graphite, NY
1 mile

Many Adirondack peaks have no trees. Some, like Treadway, once had trees. They were badly burned by fires in the late eighteen and early nineteen hundreds. These raging **fires even burned the thin soil** made up of leaf litter that had accumulated since the last ice age. The fires left these peaks as bare of soil as the glaciers did. A few mosses have returned and gradually trees will grow back. However, the process of accumulating soil is very slow so it will take a long time before there will be a forest on mountains like Treadway.

Other mountains, particularly those in the High Peaks, are so tall and the weather on their summits is so severe that no trees will grow. We say these peaks are **above tree-line**. The plants that do grow are fragile plants usually found far to the north. In these areas with **Alpine summits**, it is essential to stay on the trails and avoid trampling what few plants there are.

To mark trails on open rock, two methods are used. Sometimes arrows are painted on the rocks. At other times, small stones are heaped up into a small pile or **cairn**. Cairns are placed at intervals along the trail.

Start by heading north through the campground for fifteen minutes toward campsite 38 to find the Bear Pond Trail. Take this blue trail for 0.35 mile to an intersection. Turn left, west, here on the yellow Clear Pond Trail. This winds around the tip of North Pond to an intersection where you turn right for 0.3 mile toward the strip of land that separates Rock Pond from Little Rock Pond. Continue south on the yellow and blue Rock Pond Trail. It leads you up through a draw and down to the eastern shore of Clear Pond. Stay on the trail (a fork to the east leads back to Putnam Pond). The trail passes Mud Pond and comes to a four-way intersection with a red-marked trail.

The way east also leads to Putnam Pond. Treadway is to the west 2.2 miles away. The trail is level at first, then climbs a shoulder of Big Clear Pond Mountain. After another level stretch, the red trail begins the climb of Treadway. Much of the summit of Treadway is bare because of fires in 1910 and 1911. You quickly reach open rock so you need to follow cairns that mark the trail. Three knobs form the summit of Treadway. The first is at 4.6 miles. Here the trail turns sharply to the north toward the second knob. Beyond it, the trail turns to the west and dips into a deep valley. The last knob, 0.4 mile from the second, is Treadway's true summit.

From Treadway you can see the High Peaks and such fire tower mountains as Blue and Snowy. Views to the east include Lake Champlain and the mountains of Vermont. The walk back, retracing your steps, will take about two and a half to three hours. This all-day adventure is good preparation for even bigger climbs.

28 - The Brothers

Distance - 5.2 miles round trip, 2,200-foot vertical rise, time - 4 to 5 hours

The Brothers are a series of peaks on a long ridge overlooking the Johns Brook Valley at the edge of the High Peaks region. The southern face of the ridge is so precipitous that there are views almost all the way along the top. The trailhead is called the Garden and it is at the end of Johns Brook Road in Keene Valley. The Garden has limited parking and can be full on weekends. There is no parking along the road to the Garden, so if it is full, you must hike elsewhere.

(If the Garden Lot is full, try Noonmark, which starts from the public parking area provided by the Ausable Club. The parking area is located west of NY 73, in St. Huberts, a few miles south of Keene Valley. The trail is a good substitute for the Brothers.)

The trail to the Brothers is to the right of the Johns Brook Trail at the west end of the Garden. It is marked with

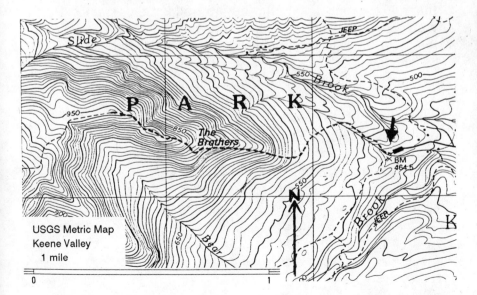

USGS Metric Map
Keene Valley
1 mile

0   1

97

Adirondack Mountain Club (ADK) markers. The trail starts climbing steeply from the Garden. Watch carefully as markers direct you around small cliffs. In the first half hour you can climb 600 feet to the first views back toward Giant. The trail continues on a narrow ridge of bare rock to the first real lookout. The trail winds around another small cliff, then separates, with the right spur giving views of Hurricane to the northeast. From the next overlook you can begin to see the peaks of the Range Trail, from Armstrong to Gothics to Saddleback and Basin.

The trail takes you briefly into the woods, then back along the edge. In places there are cliffs on both sides and at one point you scramble up through a cleft in a small cliff. Beyond there is a view to the north toward Porter with its cliffs and the Jay Range beyond Keene.

It is such fun to walk on open rock. There is a narrow cleft in the rock that you can scramble up-it has been called 'fat man's misery.' More rock walking follows, then at 1.5 miles, after an hour and twenty minutes of walking, you reach First Brother at just under 3,000 feet in elevation.

Past First Brother, the trail is level for a time, then it drops slightly, and climbs again. There is a steep rock scramble or you can take an easier route around to the right. The trail goes into the woods and leads to another view toward Porter, then comes back to the sidewalk smooth ledges on the cliff tops. These lead you to Second Brother, a knob at 3,160 feet, which is 0.25 mile from First Brother.

Beyond Second Brother, the trail is again in the woods for a short time. When it returns to open rock, you can see ahead to Third Brother. The trail drops briefly again, then climbs through a beautiful forest of paper birch. (You can recognize these trees by their white bark. Paper birch are among the first trees to come back after a fire and a tremendous fire swept the northern slopes of the Brothers.) You walk through this lovely forest for nearly half an hour.

As you emerge from the birch forest, you have spectacular views of the peaks and slides of the Range. From Third Brother at elevation 3,700 feet, you can see ahead to Big Slide with its almost vertical cliffs. At this point, turn around and head back to the Garden.

Other Big Hikes and Mountain Climbs
   Catamount 3.8 miles, round trip, 1,568-foot vertical rise
   Pitchoff 4.5 mile loop, 2,000-foot elevation change
   Ampersand 5.6 miles, round trip, 1,790-foot vertical rise
   Cascade 4.7 miles, round trip, 1,940-foot vertical rise
   Noonmark 5.3 miles, round trip, 2,277-foot vertical rise
   Descriptions of trails to these mountains are in either the
Northern or *High Peaks Discover* Guides. You will need these
descriptions to find the trailheads and to follow the trails. Read
these trail descriptions carefully. They were not written for young
people, but they were written to be as simple as possible. If you
can read and understand them and use them to hike one or
more of these trails, then you are ready for almost any day-hike in
the Adirondacks.

Directions for Driving to the Trailheads

1 - Willie Marsh. This trail straddles the southern boundary of the Park. Take NY 29A northwest from Gloversville; Willie Road is a left turn 2 miles north of Meco Road. Drive 1.8 miles along Willie Road to a parking area on the right; the trail begins on the left.

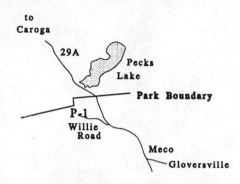

2 - Adirondack VIC at Newcomb. This new interpretive center is almost 13 miles east of Long Lake on NY 28N. It is 24.4 miles west of Northway exit 29 via the Blue Ridge Road which leads to NY 28N west. Access is also from North Creek via NY 28N.

   9 - Goodnow Mountain Trailhead is located at the center of the Park. Its trailhead is near Newcomb, 11.4 miles east of Long Lake on NY 28N and 26.5 miles or just over 1.5 miles west of the entrance to the Adirondack VIC at Newcomb.

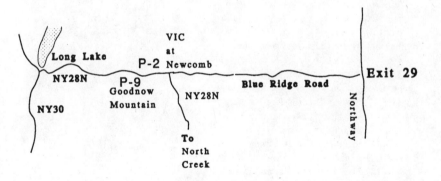

3 - Adirondack VIC at Paul Smiths. This center is in the far northern Adirondacks, north of Tupper Lake or Saranac Lake. It is 0.8 miles north of Paul Smith's College on NY 30, the principal highway bisecting the Park in a north-south direction.

4 - Cranberry Lake Boardwalk Nature Trail. NY 3 is the principal highway going east-west in the northwestern Adirondacks. Cranberry Lake is west of Tupper Lake and south of NY 3. The public Campground Road is just east of the village; the road south leads to the campground entrance on the east shore of the lake. See trail map for details.

101

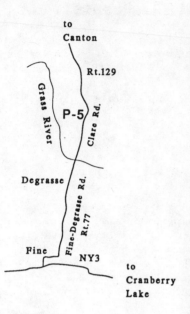

5 - Lampson Falls. The falls are in the northwestern Adirondacks between Canton and Fine, which is west of Cranberry Lake on NY 3. From Fine on NY 3, head east, then north on the Fine-Degrasse Road to Degrasse. Continue north from Degrasse on Clare Road, or County Route 77 for 4.6 miles to a sign for the Grass River Wild Forest.

14 - Rock and Long Ponds. (See map below) East Road in the village of Speculator passes the school and continues onto International Paper Company's Speculator Tree Farm Tract. This road is a seasonal road and even in summer may not be passable to ordinary cars. Many roads branch from the main road, which winds generally north across the Long Level, past the turn to the dam over the Kunjamuk River to a parking area just short of state land. The trailhead and parking area are 8 miles from Speculator.

6 - Auger Falls. Drive north on NY 30 from Wells past the intersection of NY 8 and follow NY 8 and 30 north for 1.5 miles to a dirt road on the right. The road leads to a parking area.

    7 - Jimmy Creek Waterfalls. To find Jimmy Creek, drive west on Algonquin Road from NY 30 in Wells. That road begins near the dam at the outlet of Lake Algonquin. Turn left on West River Road and follow it for just over 4 miles to a turnout where Jimmy Creek flows into the Sacandaga River.

    23 - The Northville-Placid Trail South of Whitehouse. The Whitehouse Trailhead is at the end of West River Road. Continue past Jimmy Creek to a parking area at the end of the road, 8.5 miles from NY 30 in Wells.

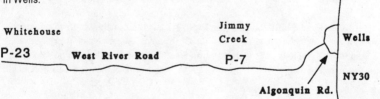

8 - Kane Mountain. Kane Mountain is east of NY 10 and 29A at Canada Lake; it is can be reached from Johnstown or Gloversville, or south on NY 10 from Piseco. Immediately north of the bridge over the channel between Green and Canada Lake on NY 10 and 29A, Green Lake Road heads north. Drive down the dirt road until it begins to curve to the right. At that point, a narrower dirt track keeps on going straight ahead. Follow it for 100 yards to the parking area. See trail map for additional information.

9 - Goodnow Mountain - see driving map for Hike 2

10 - Bass Lake. To reach the trailhead, drive east of Northway Exit 29 to NY 9 and turn north on NY 9 for 2.3 miles. Turn right toward Port Henry and within 0.15 mile, turn right again onto a narrow macadam road. The trail begins near the end of the road.

to Port Henry

P-10

Northway

NY9

Exit 29

North Hudson

11 - Mitchell Ponds. Cedar River Road heads southwest from NY 30 just west of the bridge over the Cedar River. The road is paved at first, then becomes dirt and gravel covered. At 12.3 miles, it reaches a favorite camping area at Cedar River Flow. Here the road enters the Moose River Plains. You must sign in at the register and drive slowly on the long dirt road. Follow it for 13.6 miles to a T intersection. Turn right at the intersection for 0.4 mile to the trailhead for Mitchell Ponds. After you finish your hike, you can continue driving 8.5 miles north toward Limekiln Lake and NY 28 near Inlet. This is the shortest approach to Mitchell Ponds if you start from near Old Forge.

20 - Rocky Mountain. The trail begins from NY 28, 1.2 miles east of Eagle Bay or 0.9 miles north of Inlet.

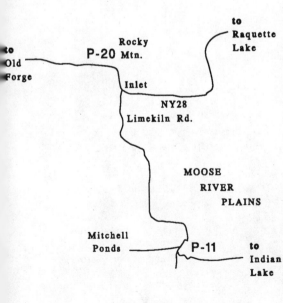

to Old Forge

P-20 Rocky Mtn.

Inlet

NY28
Limekiln Rd.

to Raquette Lake

MOOSE RIVER PLAINS

Mitchell Ponds

P-11

to Indian Lake

12 - Kibby Pond. NY 8 traverses the south-central Adirondacks in an east-west direction. The western part of the stretch between NY 30 north of Wells and NY 28 at Wevertown has few guideposts. The trailhead is on the south side of NY 8 west of Johnsburgh and 1.1 miles west of the well-marked, big Siamese Ponds Trailhead. It is 3.7 miles east of the big Shanty Brook Trailhead. (These two trailheads with their large parking areas are the most obvious guideposts along this stretch of NY 8.)

13 - Grassy and Wilson Ponds. The Adirondack Museum is on NY 30, just north of the intersection with NY 28 in Blue Mountain Lake in the heart of the Adirondacks. The trailhead is 2.8 miles west of Blue Mountain Lake on the south side of NY 28.

14 - Rock and Long Ponds - see driving map for Hike 6, Auger Falls.

15 - Clockmill Pond. To find this trailhead, you can either drive north on the Powley-Piseco Road from Stratford, or east and south on it from NY 10, just below the bridge over the outlet of Piseco Lake. Clockmill Corners is 4.3 miles from NY 10, 14.8 miles from Stratford. Access to the southern end is from either of two roads heading north from NY 29A just east of the bridge over the East Canada Creek.

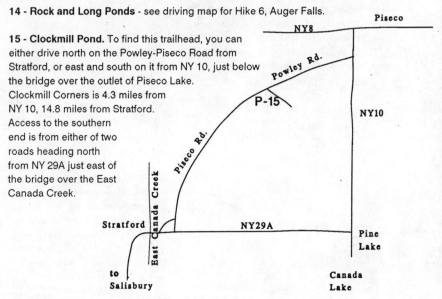

16 - Tirrell Pond. The trailhead is at the top of the hill north of the Adirondack Museum on NY 30 in Blue Mountain Lake. Tirrell Pond Trail starts at the northern end of the parking area and trailhead for Blue Mountain.

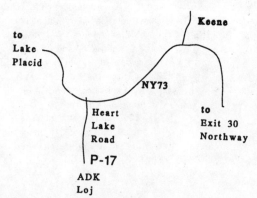

17 - Mount Jo. The High Peaks Trailhead is at the end of Adirondack Lodge Road. That road heads south from NY 73 east of Lake Placid and the Olympic ski jump or west of the VanHoevenburg Ski Center. There is a fee for parking in the Loj lot.

104

18 - Watch Hill. The beginning is on NY 30 in the long stretch between Speculator and Indian Lake. It is 3.9 miles north of the Indian Lake Islands Campground and 1.2 mile south of the parking turnout for Snowy Mountain.

19 - Deer Leap. From Northway Exit 24, head east, then turn north on NY 9N past Northwest Bay and the Clay Meadow Trailhead. The road climbs Tongue Mountain and begins to descend. The road curves to the east and nine miles north on NY 9N, you reach the parking area for Deer Leap, which is on the north side of the road, with the trailhead opposite on the south side.

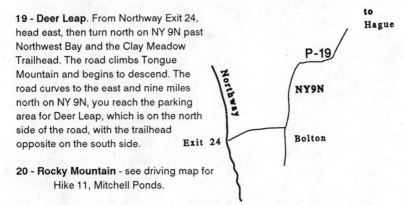

20 - Rocky Mountain - see driving map for Hike 11, Mitchell Ponds.

21 - Scarface. NY 86 connects Saranac Lake and Lake Placid, with Ray Brook between them. The trailhead for Scarface is 0.1 mile south of Ray Brook on Ray Brook Road, which heads south from NY 86 a little to the west of DEC's Region 5 and the Adirondack Park Agency buildings.

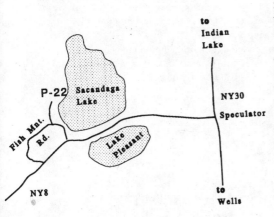

22 - Fawn Lake. To find the trailhead, you need to locate Fish Mountain Road, which loops south of NY 8 just west of Speculator and west of the signs leading to Moffit Beach Campground. From the western end of the loop, head north for 1.2 miles until you reach lakeshore, then turn left for 0.7 mile to a marked parking area at the end of the road. Signs for a lodge, Road's End, will put you on the right road, the parking area is beyond Road's End.

23 - Northville-Placid Trail South of Whitehouse - see driving map for Hike 7, Jimmy Creek Waterfalls.

105

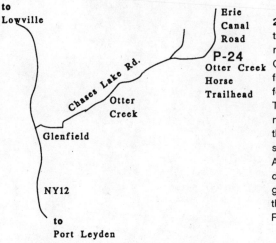

24 - Pitcher Pond. Turn east toward Gelnfield from NY 12, north of Lyons Falls. Take Chases Lake Road northeast from Glenfield, following signs for the Otter Creek Horse Trails. There is such a dense network of road and trails in this area, that it is easiest to start from the Horse Trails Assembly area, but you can drive the first part of the roads given in the trail description to the beginning of Pitcher Pond Road.

25 - The Crows. To start, take East Hill Road east from Keene. The road is just south of the intersection of NY 9N and NY 73 in Keene. Follow East Hill Road for 2.1 miles to a left fork to O'Toole Road, then continue on O'Toole Road to its end in another 1.1 miles. There is a grassy clearing here for parking.

    28 - The Brothers. Turn west on Interbrook Road in Keene Valley. The intersection is marked with a High Peaks sign. The road turns sharply right to cross Johns Brook, then climbs to the Garden Parking Area, where there is limited parking.

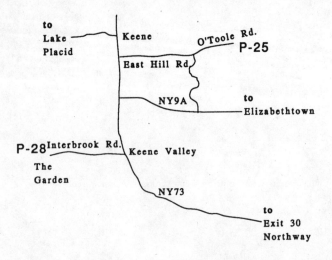

26 - Peaked Mountain. The trailhead is at the boat launch site at the foot of Thirteenth Lake. Thirteenth Lake Road heads south from NY 28, 0.5 mile west of North River. Stay right, 3.5 miles up this road for the parking lot, which is 200 yards from the lake.

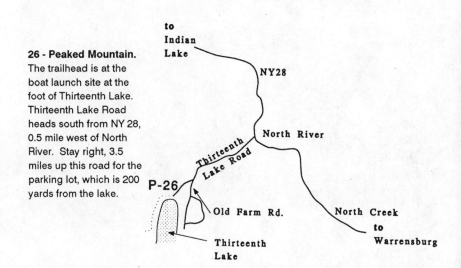

to Indian Lake

NY28

North River

Thirteenth Lake Road

P-26

Old Farm Rd.

North Creek

to Warrensburg

Thirteenth Lake

27 - Treadway. To reach Putnam Pond Campground, drive east for 13.3 miles from Northway Exit 28 on NY 74. Turn south at Chilson and follow the signs for 3.6 miles to the campground entrance. (There is a day use fee.)

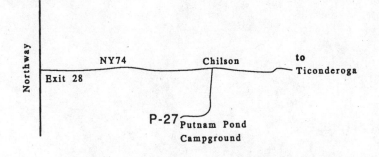

Northway

Exit 28

NY74

Chilson

to Ticonderoga

P-27 Putnam Pond Campground

28 - The Brothers - see driving map for hike 25, the Crows.

Index to Terms Used in the Guide

Barbara McMartin is the author of thirteen guidebooks and two histories. She has been writing about the Adirondacks for over two decades and during that time she has devoted herself to Adirondack causes, serving on numerous boards and committees. She was chairman of the Committee for the 1992 Adirondack Park Centennial.

The reader may want to have her *Fifty Hikes in the Adirondacks* as well as other books in the Discover Series. The regions they cover are shown on the map.

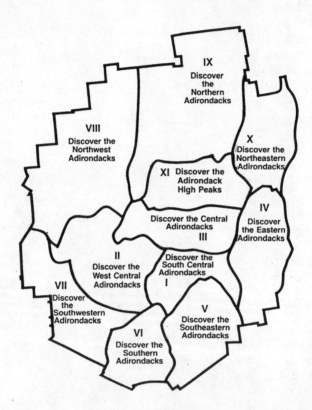

Gregory Palestri was trained in architecture and art at The Cooper Union in New York City and has done illustrations for *Adirondack Life* magazine. He currently resides inside the Blue Line with his wife and their dog and cat.

Other books written by Barbara McMartin
may be purchased at your local bookstore or from
North Country Books. These include:

Adventures in Hiking

Hides, Hemlocks and Adirondack History

Fifty Hikes in the Adirondacks

Discover the Adirondacks Series
    High Peaks
    South Central
    West Central
    Central
    Eastern
    Southeastern
    Southern
    Southwestern
    Northwestern
    Northern
    Northeastern

NORTH COUNTRY BOOKS, INC.
PUBLISHER—DISTRIBUTOR
Charlestown Complex, Box 217
311 Turner Street
Utica, New York 13501

Telephone: (315) 735-4877